PIANO COMPANION

A Comprehensive, Accelerated Approach

to

Learning How To Play The Piano

by

Note, Chord Symbol And Ear

DAVE CLARK

PIANO COMPANION: A Comprehensive, Accelerated Approach to Learning How To Play The Piano by Note, Chord Symbol And Ear

Printed in the U.S.A. by
Southern Heritage Press
PO Box 10937
St. Petersburg, Florida 33733
813-821-22379

All inquiries should be addressed to: Dave Clark
403 N. Bryan Circle
Brandon, FL 33511

ISBN: 0-941072-18-5

Acknowledgments

I would like to thank the following people for their outstanding work in helping me prepare this book for publication:

Daniel Swartwood, for tirelessly "taking it on the chops" to create the computerized transcription of all the text and musical examples in this book;

Margaret Clark, for happily and patiently contributing a comprehensive index;

Julia Moseley, for her patience and time in the editing process;

LeGrand and Pallard, for the incredible cover photography;

Mark Fragos, for the astounding cover graphics design which dared to "improve upon the perfection" of the original photograph.

I would especially like to thank those who sowed the seeds of my interest in music. This book is the fruit of their support:

My sister, Susan, who realized that our childhood home should contain a piano;

My mother, Anne, who listened to countless hours of piano practice;

My father, Hugh, who remains my favorite piano student;

My present and former students, who by their enthusiasm and curiosity have challenged me to create new ways to present the musical learning experience.

Finally, I would like to thank my bride, Marie, who initiated the idea for this book...yet another way it seems like my life was just waiting for you.

AUTHOR'S NOTE

Though this book is designed for self-instruction, it is not my intention to have it function in the place of a piano instructor. I heartily recommend that anyone using this book, do so in combination with piano lessons. A book is somewhat limited in its ability to keep people on task, and is one way communication; monologue instead of dialogue. Piano lessons will make up for these and other limitations and, at the same time, speed up your learning.

PREFACE

Although there are three ways to play the piano, conventional piano lessons provide instruction on only one: by note. The results are less than desirable. Many outstanding piano students become disinterested and quit taking lessons. Many piano students of average ability, studying piano as a hobby, decide they've maxed out and quit taking lessons. In short, large numbers of piano students are replacing their love for the study of piano with disillusionment.

Conventional piano lessons consist of little more than processing dots on lines and spaces because:

1.) Conventional teaching methods continue to produce conventional piano teachers.

2.) Piano students are not aware that they can avail themselves to three directions of study.

It is my intention, through this book, to transform conventional teaching methods from "one way" study to "three way" study, thereby allowing students not only a more comprehensive approach to learning how to play the piano, but also a much more enjoyable learning experience.

Besides being played by note, the piano may be played by chord symbol or by ear. Most piano teachers think playing the piano by chord symbol consists of having the right hand play a melody line while the left hand pounds out chords.These piano teachers are sadly misinformed and behind the times.Like playing by note, playing the piano by chord symbol was elevated to an art form a very long time ago.Many of these same piano teachers are responsible for promulgating the notion that playing the piano by ear is somehow bad or undesirable. Nothing could be further from the truth.

It's easy to point out people who have developed, of necessity on their own, only rudimentary chord symbol or ear skills. We call them wham-slam-bang pianists. While their current performance skills are inferior, we must remember that the beginning note reading student's current performance skills are also inferior. When we, as piano teachers, expand our own abilities so that we may make available formal chord symbol and ear instruction, then the wham-slam-bang pianists will have an opportunity to transform themselves. Only then will the "by note" snobbery subside.

It all boils down to this: When you, as a piano student, are paying someone to teach you how to play the piano, your personal musical interests and the overall direction of study should be open to discussion — not left entirely up to the piano teacher. If your piano teacher is teaching you only by note, you are receiving only one-third of what you are paying for. Don't let a teacher with limited abilities limit the development of your own abilities.

I know this book conveys what some people would consider radical ideas. However, it is my sincere desire that you find it a helpful, enticing and soft-spoken partner (a sort of "piano compãgno") in your quest to learn the opportunities which exist for you on a piano keyboard.

DAVE CLARK

TABLE OF CONTENTS

CHAPTER ONE – THREE OPPORTUNITIES   1

   The "As Written" Approach 2
   The "Chord Symbol" Approach 3
   The "Ear Approach" 4
   Combining The Three Ways 5

CHAPTER TWO – BEGINNER PERFORMANCE   6

   Starting Out 6
   Keyboard Chart 7
   Slogans 8
   Note Relationships 8
   Flash Cards 10
   Sharps, Flats And Naturals 10
   Scales And Key Signatures 12
   What To Practice 15
   About Practice 15
   Basic Practice Techniques 16
   The Pedals 28
   Symbols And Terms 30
   Practice Hints 32
   A Special Note To Parents Of Piano Students 33

CHAPTER THREE – BEGINNER THEORY   35

   Intervals 35
   Chords 35
   Rhythm 39

CHAPTER FOUR – BEGINNER EAR   40

   Intervals 40
   Chords 40

CHAPTER FIVE – INTERMEDIATE PERFORMANCE _____ 42

    What To Practice 42
    The Divided Line 42
    Dotted Eight Sixteenths 43
    Triplets 44
    Two Hand Method 45
    Three Hand Method 48
    Arpeggiation Method 60
    Scales 63
    The Marathon Scale 70
    Sight Reading 71
    Memorization 73
    Now...About Technique 75
    Embellishments 78

CHAPTER SIX – INTERMEDIATE THEORY _____ 82

    Lowered Intervals 82
    Chords 82
    Special Instruction Chords 86
    Music Systems 89
    Circle Of Fifths 89
    Relative Minor/Relative Major 92
    A Short Cut 94
    Practical Applications Of The Circle Of Fifths 95
    Figured Bass 96
    Scale Degrees 97
    Replacement Chords 98
    Practical Application Of Figured Bass 99
    Mutations 101
    Mutations And The Three Forms Of Minor 102
    Altered Scale Degree Mutation 104
    Secondary Dominant Mutations 105
    Using Figured Bass For Transposition 107
    Modulation 107
    Music Construction 111
    Creating Melody 111
    Building Harmony 114
    "As Written" Harmonization 114
    "Chord Symbol" Harmonization 118
    Songform 119
    Development 120
    A Sales Pitch About Construction Your Own Music . . . 121

CHAPTER SEVEN – INTERMEDIATE EAR _____ 122

Lowered Intervals 122
Three Common Seventh Chords 122
Playing By Ear 123

CHAPTER EIGHT – ADVANCED THEORY _____ 128

Voicing 128
Chord Scales 128
Special Instruction Chords 131
Altered Tones 139
Scale Degree Personalities 141
Non-Harmonic Tones And Resolving Devices 152
Modes 167
Do I Really Need To Know This Stuff? 177

CHAPTER NINE – ADVANCED PERFORMANCE _____ 178

"As Written" Approach 178
Adaptation 178
"Chord Symbol" Approach 180
Chord Scale Improvisation 181
Pre-Hearing 185
Non-Harmonic Tone Improvisation 186
Summary Of The "Chord Symbol" Approach 191

CHAPTER TEN – ADVANCED EAR _____ 194

Jazz Improvisation And Modal Improvisation 194
Transcription 194
Thematic Development 197
Composer's Disease And Composer's Dilemma 209

CHAPTER ELEVEN – A SHORT BIOGRAPHY OF THE PIANO _____ 212

**CHAPTER TWELVE – AN OPEN LETTER TO PIANO TEACHERS
AND PIANO STUDENTS** _____ 213

APPENDIX – I.   THE CLASSIFICATION OF INTERVALS _____ 216
Why Are Perfect Intervals Called "Perfect"? . . 217
II.   JAZZ/MODAL IMPROVISATION TRANSCRIPTIONS
Example One 219
Example Two 222
III.   MUSIC STYLES/TYPES/PERIODS CHECKLIST . . 227
INDEX – _____ 229

My best teachers reduced things to their simplest, most logical terms.

CHAPTER ONE
THREE OPPORTUNITIES

There are three ways to play the piano: by note, by chord symbol, and by ear.

When a person plays by note, he reads the little dots on a page of music. These dots are located either on lines or spaces. When a note head has a line running through it, it is said to be a "line note".

Note Stem ☞

Note Head ☞

When a note head sits between lines, it is said to be a "space note".

Each line or space corresponds with a note on the keyboard. This is how musicians read notes: by learning which dot corresponds with which note on the keyboard. We call this way of playing "as written" or "by note".

When a person plays by chord symbol, he reads the letters, numbers and symbols on a page of music, usually with a single line of notes. When included in written music, chord symbols are found just above the notes.

A chord symbol might be as simple as: C

Or it could be a bit more involved: $C^{\sharp}m\ Z^{(\flat 9)}$ over E

There are about forty common chord symbols and each represents a particular group of notes.

When a person plays by ear, he reads nothing. Instead he listens for every note he plays. However, it should be understood that various music systems are sometimes used to help a person find the right notes.

All types of music can be played using any one (or combination) of the three ways. No one way of playing the piano is THE way or the best way. Each offers advantages and disadvantages. Let's look more closely at the characteristics of each.

THE "AS WRITTEN" APPROACH

Of the three ways to play the piano, the "as written" approach calls for the least amount of abstract reasoning. This is because each note is written exactly where it "belongs". How a composer wants his notes to be played (i.e. quickly, loudly, slowly, softly, etc.) may also be written into the music. Consequently, precise repetition of a performance is most easily accomplished through the use of the "as written" approach. However, because a "by note" musician must process larger quantities of written information (than the "chord symbol" musician or the "ear" musician), most people find the "as written" approach the most challenging way to learn to play the piano. Usually, more preparation time is necessary for an "as written" performance. Because more written information must be processed when performing as written, the process of learning to read music on sight (called "sight-reading") takes much longer to develop and remains more difficult than "chord symbol" sight-reading. (Obviously, sight-reading does not exist in the "by ear" approach.)

To perform, the "as written" musician must either read music that is written on paper, or memorize music that is written on paper. For the person who has learned to play only by note, "paper music" is both necessary and constraining.

The vast majority of piano teachers know how to play only by note and consequently, teach only by note. These teachers tend to emphasize and develop the mechanical aspects of performance, while disregarding pleasant aesthetic growth. The "as written" approach <u>can</u> provide pleasant aesthetic growth, especially when taught in conjunction with the "chord symbol" approach and the "ear" approach.

I recommend learning <u>only</u> by note until an intermediate level of performance has been achieved. Then, while continuing to improve your note reading skills, introduce yourself to the "chord symbol" approach. Because "as written" calls for the most self-discipline, it deserves a head start over the other ways to play.

For the most part, classical music and ragtime music are most easily accessed using the "as written" approach.

THE "CHORD SYMBOL" APPROACH

The "chord symbol" approach offers a musician some freedom to create while he plays. The first part of this approach consists of three methods which are used to combine some of what is written with some of what is heard. This combining of what is written with what is heard is easier to learn than the "as written" approach because much less written information has to be processed.

The three methods used in the "chord symbol" approach are "Two Hand Method", "Three Hand Method" and "Arpeggiation Method". If these methods had not been developed, the "chord symbol" approach would require such a large amount of abstract reasoning that, for most people, it would be much more difficult than the "as written" approach.

When playing by chord symbol, the melody is read by note, while the harmony is partially read via the chord symbol and partially done by ear. The rhythm of the melody is read, while the rhythm of the harmony is done almost entirely by ear.

The three methods mentioned lead to the more advanced forms of chord symbol performance: Chord Scale Improvisation, Non-Harmonic Tone Improvisation and Jazz/Modal Improvisation. These three types of improvisation require well developed, keenly perceptive aural ability and, as such, can really be considered a combination of the "chord symbol" approach and the "ear" approach.

To perform, the beginning "chord symbol" musician must either read music that is written on paper, or memorize music that is written on paper. However, as the "chord symbol" musician advances into the three types of improvisation, "paper music" gradually becomes unnecessary. By now you've probably guessed: The "chord symbol" approach is an ideal stepping stone to get from playing by note to playing by ear. It requires approximately one-third of the written information that is necessary for "as written" performance, and can be used either to simplify musical arrangements or to greatly enhance and enrich musical arrangements.

Because the "chord symbol approach demands more self-discipline than the "ear" approach, I recommend getting at least to the intermediate level of "chord symbol" performance before initiating any playing by ear.

For the most part, all types of popular music are most easily accessed using the "chord symbol" approach.

THE "EAR" APPROACH

The "ear" approach offers a musician complete freedom to create while he plays. For most people, learning to play by ear is not extremely challenging. Practice consists of ear training exercises and aural doodling — goofing around with whatever one chooses. Since goofing around comes naturally to most of us, getting better at playing by ear is big fun and calls for very little self-discipline.

An "ear" musician performs his own compositions or anybody else's music in any way and in any style he is able to hear. Whatever innate aural ability he lacks is often compensated for through the study and subsequent use of music systems. (Music systems are covered in chapters six, eight, nine and ten of this book.) Because no "paper music" is involved, music seems to miraculously come forth from the hands of an "ear" musician.

"Ear" musicians enjoy aural freedom. Certain "paper music" is almost impossible to find, and it is sometimes months before music which is heard on a popular radio station, at the movie theatre or on television is put on paper to be sold in stores. A person who plays by ear isn't bothered by this because his ears are his music.

There is widespread antipathy toward playing by ear. Some is well-justified in that most people who play only by ear are shallow musicians. However, I would like to suggest that people who play only by note are every bit as limited in their musical ability as people who play only by ear, though in vastly different ways.

I have never known an "ear only" musician who did not, at sometime in our musical relationship, indicate a desire to learn how to play by note. Conversely, every "as written only" musician I have ever known has, at some time or another, been intrigued at the prospect of learning how to play by ear. Indeed, there is often mild jealously and envy between these two types of musicians. When musical training, worldwide, incorporates an "ear" approach with an "as written" approach, using a "chord symbol" approach to bridge the gap between the two, this situation will no longer exist.

Ear is what music is all about — it is indeed the essence of music. By including comprehensive aural training in the learning environment, the student grasps a more thorough understanding of music and what it means to be a musician.

COMBINING THE THREE WAYS

Each way you learn to play the piano supports the others. You will spot patterns in "as written" music you would never have noticed had you not learned the "chord symbol" approach. Noticing these patterns will allow you to learn "as written" music much faster and memorize it much more easily. Your ear is a great memorization device for both "as written" and "chord symbol" music. The "as written" approach helps the process of learning to play by ear by allowing the musician to visualize melody, harmony and rhythm in ways he otherwise would be incapable of. The "chord symbol" approach facilitates learning how to play by ear for anyone who, for years, has been stuck in the note reading rut.

The bottom line is this: A complete keyboard musician is able to perform all three ways. He is able to rise to any performing situation comfortably. The complete keyboard musician realizes he is well-equipped to enjoy his music. He indulges in creating music for himself and others. Whether you are a piano hobbyist, piano student, piano teacher or an aspiring concert pianist, becoming a complete keyboard musician is to your advantage, both as a listener and as a performer.

It saddens me to tell you that the vast majority of people teaching piano are not complete keyboard musicians. By relating only what they know, their limitations become your limitations. Choose your teachers carefully. You will probably have to learn the "as written" approach from one teacher, the "chord symbol" approach from another and the "ear" approach from still another. It is worth the search. This book is written to make you aware of the opportunities that exist for you on the piano keyboard, and to teach you as well as a book is able.

CHAPTER TWO
<u>BEGINNER PERFORMANCE</u>

<u>STARTING OUT</u>

To begin learning the piano, take your left hand index finger and strike the left-most note on the piano keyboard. While holding this note down, say "A". Move to the next white note, saying "B". Keep on playing only white notes until you get to "G". Instead of going to "H", say "A" again. Go on to B, C, D, E, F, G, A, B, C, and so on right up to the top of the keyboard. If the last note you say is "C", you did just fine.

Now, let's look at the black notes. The piano keyboard is laid out with a series of black note groupings. The black notes alternate in groups of two, then three and so on. To find any C note on the piano is easy. First, find any any black note grouping of two notes. Then play the white note just to the left. This note will always be a C. Middle C is the note we will use as a starting point, and it is found by going to the C closest to your piano's trade mark. Middle C is not the center of the piano keyboard, just the middle-most C on the keyboard.

Middle C is written as a line note, meaning it has a line running through the center of its head. It sits just below the treble clef staff when the right hand plays it, and just above the bass clef staff when the left hand is supposed to play it. It has its own little line called a "ledger line".

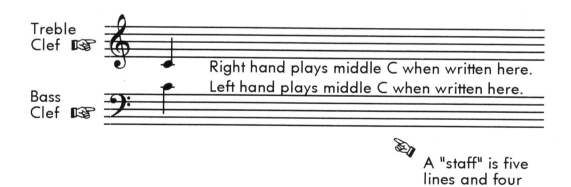

Treble Clef ☞

Right hand plays middle C when written here.
Left hand plays middle C when written here.

Bass Clef ☞

A "staff" is five lines and four spaces.

(Please note: the plural for "staff" is "staves".)

KEYBOARD CHART

As a beginner, note reading is what you are all about. There are three ways to learn how to read the notes — if you don't count the fourth way.

The first way is called a keyboard chart. It is simply a note dictionary in picture form. Here is a keyboard chart with some accompanying terms. By the way, don't bother to memorize musical terms. Using them is enough to remember them.

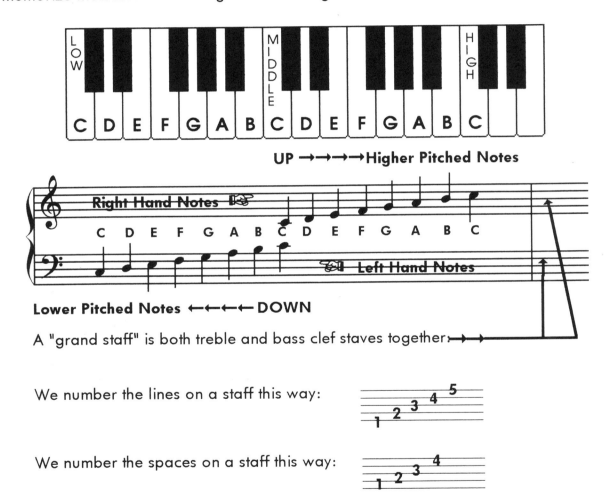

UP →→→→Higher Pitched Notes

Right Hand Notes 🖎

C D E F G A B C D E F G A B C

🖎 **Left Hand Notes**

Lower Pitched Notes ←←←← DOWN

A "grand staff" is both treble and bass clef staves together →→

We number the lines on a staff this way:

We number the spaces on a staff this way:

To use a keyboard chart, simply determine the line or space number of the note you are looking up. Then find the note on the grandstaff of the keyboard chart and follow above the note, up to the picture of the keyboard. You may now find the note on your own piano keyboard by counting up or down from middle C. You're doing super. Hang in there!

SLOGANS

The second way to learn how to read notes is called slogans. This is a very old-fashioned way.

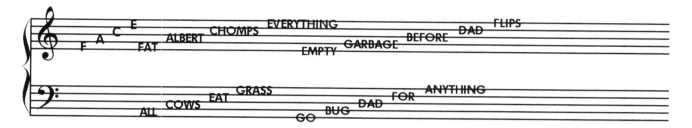

To find a note using the slogans, use the starting letter of the word that falls on a particular line or space. Be careful not to confuse the treble clef slogans with the bass clef slogans.

NOTE RELATIONSHIPS

Before we cover the third way to read notes, let's look more closely at the first two ways. They work well, yet they both are two step processes. What I mean is you must 1.) look up the note and then 2.) find it on the keyboard. Would it be easier if we could reduce the note reading procedure to a one step process? You bet!

The third way is this one step procedure. It is the way you will end up reading notes, no matter which way you choose to learn. It is the way all professional musicians read notes. Do you really think the pros think letters when they're reading the dots we call notes? No way! They read notes in relation to each other! The third way is called note relationships.

When a note reader goes from a line note up to the next line note, he just skips one white note on the keyboard. The white note he is skipping is the space note in between.

Likewise, when a note reader goes from a space note up to the next space note, he just skips one white note on the keyboard.

Quite obviously, this works when a note reader is going from a line note down to the next line note or from a space note down to the next space note. He just skips one white note.

When a note reader is going from a line note up to the next space note, he doesn't skip any notes. He just goes up to the next white note.

Likewise, when a note reader is going from a space note up to the next line note, he doesn't skip any notes. He just goes up to the next white note.

Quite obviously, this works when a note reader is going from a line note down to the next space note or from a space note down to the next line note. He doesn't skip any white notes.

So what you want to remember is:

> line to line - skip one
>
> space to space - skip one
>
> line to space - skip none
>
> space to line - skip none

Reading notes this way, all you have to do is figure out the first note of the song from a keyboard chart or a slogan (or your good memory) and read the second note in relation to the first, the third in relation to the second, the fourth in relation to the third, and so on till the song is done!

FLASH CARDS

The fourth way of learning to read notes is really a note reading aid. Go to your neighborhood music store and buy a set of music flash cards. From the whole deck of cards, pull out the eight bass clef notes from middle C down to 2nd space C. Then pull out the eight treble clef cards from middle C up to 3rd space C. You should be holding a total of sixteen flash cards. Simply practice saying them until you can get through all sixteen cards in twenty seconds. This might take several months. Enjoy the challenge! Learning to say the flash cards is a supporting method for learning to play the flash cards. Playing them is much more important. When you tire of saying the cards, practice playing the cards by setting them in front of you on the piano and removing each card as the note is found and played on the keyboard. Obviously, it helps to shuffle the cards from time to time! Practice playing the cards until you can get through all sixteen cards in thirty seconds. You might get someone to set them down in front of you, as you play them, so you are able to use both hands.

Some final words of caution concerning learning how to read notes: using the finger numbers to help you find notes on the piano, as a replacement for actually learning to read the notes, is a dead end street. Why? Quite obviously, not all music can be performed using ten notes (one for each finger) and one hand position. If you find yourself reading the finger numbers instead of reading the notes, use some typewriter correction fluid to paint over at least some of the numbers.

SHARPS, FLATS AND NATURALS

To learn to read the black notes, you must understand sharps and flats. A sharp sign (#) placed before a note tells you to go up (to the right) one note. This will usually put you on a black note.

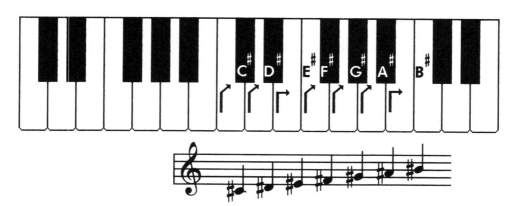

A flat (b) sign placed before a note tells you to go down (to the left) one note. This will usually put you on a black note.

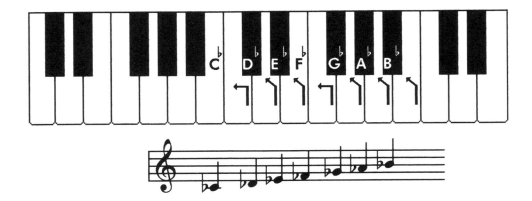

A sharped note will remain sharped until the next bar line:

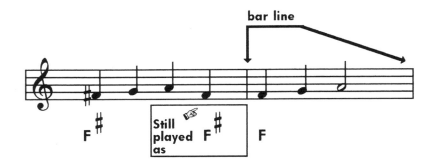

(The same holds true for flatted notes.)

To cancel a sharp or flat before the bar line, a natural sign ♮ is used:

Sharps, flats and naturals are collectively referred to as "accidentals".

SCALES AND KEY SIGNATURES

Learning scales will help orient you to the notes used in any particular song. Scales are made up of half steps and whole steps. A half step is simply two notes with <u>no</u> notes in between. To go up or down a half step, go up or down to the next note, whether black or white. For example: F# is a half step up from F and Fb is a half step down from F. A whole step is simply two notes with <u>one</u> note in between. The note in between could be black or white. For example: G is a whole step up from F and Eb is a whole step down from F.

The most commonly used scale is <u>major</u>. Here is the pattern for all major scales:

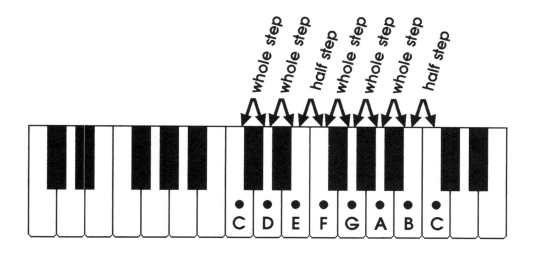

We abbreviate the pattern this way: W W H W W W H
Since we started the pattern on the note C, we have formed the C major scale. Now let's start the pattern on G to form the G major scale:

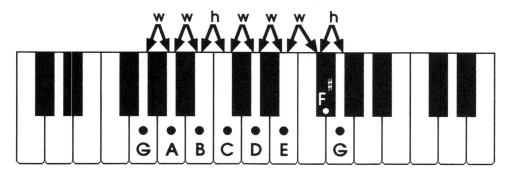

Notice that when we start on G, the pattern includes the note F#.

Here's the pattern starting on D:

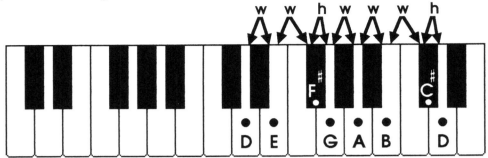

Notice the D major scale includes two sharps.

Here's the pattern starting on A:

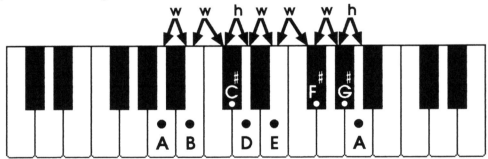

Notice the A major scale includes three sharps.

Here's the pattern starting on E:

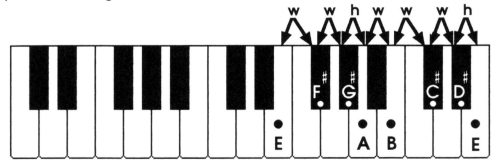

Notice the E major scale includes four sharps.

The composer uses a key signature to tell you which scale he used when he wrote the song. The key signature is found to the right of the clef signs.

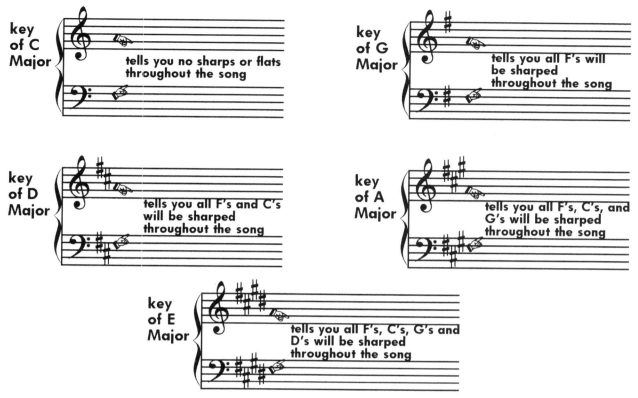

Since knowing scales will help orient you to the notes used in any particular song, I highly recommend learning them. To learn scales, you must first understand the finger numbers. Here they are:

> "**1**" indicates the thumb should be used.
> "**2**" indicates the index finger should be used.
> "**3**" indicates the middle finger should be used.
> "**4**" indicates the ring finger should be used.
> "**5**" indicates the pinky should be used.

The finger pattern is identical for the C, G, D, A, and E scales. The right hand will cross the thumb under when going up, and cross the third finger over when coming down.

The left hand will cross the third finger over when going up, and cross the thumb under when coming down.

Learn the scales hands separately, then hands together.

WHAT TO PRACTICE

For beginner level music, I recommend the <u>Belwin Piano Method</u> (Book One and Book Two) and the <u>Michael Aaron Piano Course</u> (Grade One and Grade Two). All four of these books are published by Belwin Mills. Also, <u>Edna Mae Burnam's Piano Course</u> (Book One and Book Two), published by Willis Music Company. For beginner level technical exercises, I recommend <u>A Dozen A Day</u> (Book One), published by Willis Music Company. These books will be sufficient to take you to the low intermediate level.

Don't let your teacher make you play every song in these books or any other books you or he might choose. Skip over and come back to songs. No system on the market today is so universally accommodating that every song should be played in exact order for the student to acquire the knowledge he desires. A teacher is not taking into account your learning rate when he asks you to turn the page and play the next song in the book. Everyone learns at a different rate and you should be allowed to skip songs that will teach you the same things you already know. Don't let a music teacher just plug you into his ways. Persuade him to be flexible. If he won't bend to accommodate your learning rate, fire him. Find another. Your enthusiasm to learn must be answered by the teacher accelerating his teaching methods, or else you are wasting time.

ABOUT PRACTICE

This leads us to another point. Any teacher will tell you to practice. "Practice, practice, practice!" Do you know you are not paying him to tell you to practice? Practicing is your own responsibility. Your piano teacher's job is to tell you <u>how</u> to practice. You will find teachers everywhere who will tell you <u>what</u> to practice, <u>where</u> to practice, <u>who</u> should practice, <u>when</u> to practice, <u>why</u> you should practice and <u>how much</u> you should practice. And it is a very rare teacher who will tell you <u>how</u> to practice. This rare type of teacher knows that the real teacher is the student. The piano student actually teaches himself how to play the piano when he practices. The piano teacher teaches the student <u>how</u> to practice, i.e. <u>how</u> to spend time efficiently and effectively.

I will now share with you the <u>basic practice techniques</u> used by beginner and professional alike. This is the <u>how</u> of practice. This is the most important aspect to know about practice because it is the most useful.

Let's begin with a definition of practice.

Practice: working on what you don't know.
Now, lets define playing.
Playing: working on what you do know.

You cannot play and practice the piano simultaneously. Playing is great; it boosts the ego; it's fun to rest on your laurels; it's nice to hear the old material you've already learned; and it's not practice. Playing is playing!

To practice, you should be working on the next challenge. To know what the next challenge is, you should have a guide. Here it is:

BASIC PRACTICE TECHNIQUES

1.) Hands Separate – Learn the notes.
2.) Hands Separate – Learn the fingers.
3.) Hands Separate – Learn the rhythm.
4.) Hands Together – Learn the notes.
5.) Hands Together – Learn the fingers.
6.) Hands Together – Learn the rhythm.
7.) Practice problem spots in small sections.
8.) Add shading.

Unless you are able to sight-read the piece of music, you will find these eight steps are the fastest and easiest path to learning any particular piece of music. Let's cover each individually.

1.) <u>Hands Separate</u> – <u>Learn the notes</u>. Simply go through the song, working only one hand at a time. Spend approximately the same amount of time with each hand and look for note patterns. Noticing note patterns will allow you to read a group of notes as if they were one unit. Here is an example:

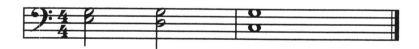

Rather than reading each note individually, notice the pattern — the top note stays the same while the bottom note goes down one. You can now play these six notes as one unit.

Since the right hand usually contains the melody, you will find yourself wanting to spend more time with it. This is partly because your ear can readily hear the melody and this makes the right hand notes much easier to learn.

I've heard people say they thought the right hand was easier to learn because they were right handed. This is not true. Handed-ness has nothing to do with learning the piano. I'm a lefty. It has never helped or hindered my learning and my right hand can do things on the piano keyboard that my left hand only dreams about doing. Many pianists complain about their "bum" left hand; the others are lying. So be forewarned: The left hand starts out at an aural disadvantage and will never catch up to the right hand's technical ability. The reason is the right hand contains more fast notes (the melody) and usually a portion of the harmony, so it consistently has to handle (fingle?) more notes and faster notes. Combine this with the aural advantage, and your left hand never stood a chance. Even if you were to tie your right hand behind your back for a year, working your left hand like crazy, your right hand would quickly regain its advantage because of the way notes and rhythms are delegated between the hands.

2.) <u>Hands Separate</u> – <u>Learn the fingers</u>. When you start out on the piano, you will have a "set hand position". This means you will set your fingers on certain notes, at the beginning of the song, and never have to move them to different notes during the playing of the song. Each finger has its note that it plays. During this stage of learning, your only concerns with the fingers are making sure your "set hand position" does not shift, and being sure to strike the notes with your fingertips. Do not allow yourself to play flat-handed. Bend your fingers! This allows each finger to work completely independent of the others.

To understand what I mean by "finger tip", point your index finger out in front of you. Now move it towards the nearest wall. The part that touches the wall is the same part that should touch the piano keyboard.

To understand what I mean by "flat-handed", lay your hand flat on a table top. This hand position does not work on the piano because: 1.) Your thumb can't stand ready and waiting on a note. Moving your hand in and out so the thumb can play its notes is wasted movement. 2.) Your pinky finger will not operate independent of the hand. The whole forearm, hand and fifth finger will go up and down with each note the fifth finger plays. This is wasted movement and wasted effort — too much meat moving up and down. 3.) The weight of the arm and hand is on the fingers: Lazy hand position. The piano keyboard is not a place to rest your hands. It is a place to work out your fingers — to develop strength, endurance and control in the five appendages of each hand. With the slow notes you play when first learning the piano, you might be tempted to say "who cares?". When you get to the faster notes at the intermediate and advanced level you will definitely be glad I cared enough to tell you now, while you are forming hand position and finger habits. Learning is easy. Un-learning and re-learning are difficult.

To understand what I mean by "bend your fingers", think of the last time you dug with your hands on the beach building a sandcastle. The claw shape that your hands naturally assume to dig in the sand is the <u>same</u> position your hands should be in over the piano keyboard. Notice your knuckles will be slightly higher than your wrist. Playing softly will take the weight of the arm and hand off the fingers, allowing you easily to maintain this hand position. Watch those pinkies, because if they stay bent, all the other fingers will bend too. I used all these words because **HAND AND FINGER POSITION ARE SUPER IMPORTANT!**

The hand and finger position I just described is not the only way pianists play. It is, however, the best way to start because all other hand and finger positions are more easily acquired after this first one becomes comfortable. By the way, if you don't clip your fingernails, when you play the piano, you'll sound like a dog running on a sidewalk.

As you get more advanced, you will be playing more notes in each song. This means your hands will leave the "set hand position" to reach these notes. The finger numbers written above and below the notes become very important. Without them, you can easily run out of fingers. Wrong fingering makes for wrong notes, wrong rhythms and lousy phrasing. The fingering which is provided is not always the best or easiest pattern. It's a composer's or an arranger's idea of the way he thinks will work the best. If you find an alternate finger pattern that is comfortable for you, it might be acceptable and work better for you.

To determine whether an alternate finger pattern is acceptable, simply notice where your fingers cross under each other or over each other. Fingers 2,3 or 4 are allowed to cross over the thumb and, conversely, the thumb is allowed to cross under fingers 2,3 or 4. Any other cross-overs or cross-unders are unacceptable. Also, consider the phrasing (note grouping) when determining alternate finger patterns: Your "new" fingering should not interrupt the flow of any group of notes. When a group of notes is slurred (played in a connected manner), your fingering should not produce any separation between the notes within that phrase.

Some music has little or no fingering provided. Feel free to take a pencil and write in the "key" fingers so your finger patterns will be reproduced the same way each time.

3.) <u>Hands Separate</u> – <u>Learn the rhythm</u>. This is the step everyone likes to skip. Once the notes and fingers are comfortable hands separate, people get impatient to hear what the song is going to sound like hands together. A little patience here goes a long way.

When you work the rhythm, work only the rhythm. In other words, don't concern yourself with stopping and going back to get a wrong note or finger. When you worked on the notes, you didn't concern yourself with a steady beat. When you worked on notes, you worked only on notes. So, when you work on rhythm, work only on rhythm. Do what you're doing, while you're doing it! After you can go through a page or two, with the exact rhythm, then you may go back to the spots you noticed had note or finger problems and work <u>just those spots </u>for notes, fingers and rhythm simultaneously. This is called "section work" and is explained in detail in step 7 of the basic practice techniques.

To learn the rhythm hands separate, you must first learn how to write in the counting using one of the following rhythm charts. To use the rhythm charts, you must understand measures, time signatures, note/rest names and note/rest values.

A measure is the distance between bar lines. Measures divide music into convenient, bite-size chunks.

A time signature is found after the key signature and before the first note of the song.

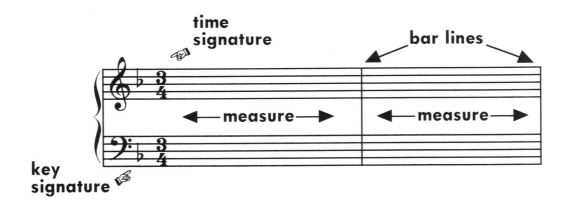

The top number of a time signature always tells you the number of beats (counts) in each measure. In the example, there are three beats in each measure. The bottom number always tells you the type of note that gets one beat. In the example a quarter note (♩) gets one beat. The most common time signature is ($\frac{4}{4}$), also written as (**C**). <u>Notes get their names from their relationship to the measure</u>. The most common measure contains four beats ($\frac{4}{4}$ time), so a quarter note (♩) gets one quarter of a measure, which is one beat. A half note (♩) gets one half of a measure, which is two beats. A whole note (o) gets the whole measure, which is four beats. The number of beats (counts) a note gets is said to be its "value".

A rest tells you not to play for a specified number of beats. A quarter rest (𝄽) gets one quarter of a measure, which is one beat. A half rest (▬) gets half of a measure, which is two beats. A whole rest (▬) gets the whole measure, which is four beats. The number of beats (counts) a rest gets is said to be its "value".

A dot (·) after any note or rest means half again the value of whatever note or rest it follows. So, a dotted half note (♩.) will get three beats. The half note itself gets two beats, plus the value of the dot, which in this case is one beat (half of two), equals a grand total of three beats. A dotted quarter note (♩.) will get 1 1/2 beats. The quarter note itself gets one beat, plus the value of the dot, which in this case is 1/2 beat (half of one), equals a grand total of 1 1/2 beats. Simple!

QUARTER LEVEL RHYTHM CHART

For notes and rests that are divisible by one quarter of the measure (one beat).

Type Of Note	Type Of Rest	Number Of Beats	Number Of Symbols Written	Actual Counting Written In Is: (Depending on which beat of the measure the note or rest enters)
o	▬	4	4 →	1 2 3 4
♩.	▬·	3	3 →	1 2 3 or 2 3 4
♩	▬	2	2 →	1 2 or 2 3 or 3 4
♩	𝄽	1	1 →	1 or 2 or 3 or 4

This rhythm level chart is very easily adapted to any time signature with 4 as its bottom number. Use it for $\frac{2}{4}$, $\frac{3}{4}$, $\frac{4}{4}$ and $\frac{6}{4}$. (In $\frac{6}{4}$ time an additional note and rest are used: o · = six beats; ▬· = six beats.)

The counting is written in between the treble and bass staves and applies to both at the same time. Here is an example:

Since the counting lines up with both hands, you may use either staff to write in the counting. However, since the right hand usually contains more notes, most people use the treble staff notes to line up their counting.

Now, let's bring eighth notes (♪ , ♫) and eighth rests (𝄾) into the picture. An eighth of a measure is 1/2 beat, so each eighth note or eighth rest will get 1/2 beat. Notice we are not dealing with the quarter level when half beats are being used. Instead, we are now at the eighth level.

EIGHTH LEVEL RHYTHM CHART

For notes and rests that are divisible by one eighth of the measure (1/2 beat).

Type Of Note	Type Of Rest	Number Of Beats	Number Of Symbols Written	Actual Counting Written In Is: (Depending on which beat of the measure the note or rest enters)
𝅝	▬	4	8 →	1 + 2 + 3 + 4 +
𝅗𝅥·	▬·	3	6 →	1 + 2 + 3 + or 2 + 3 + 4 +
𝅗𝅥	▬	2	4 →	1 + 2 + or 2 + 3 + or 3 + 4 +
𝅘𝅥·	𝄽·	1 1/2	3 →	1 + 2 or + 2 + or 2 + 3 etc.
𝅘𝅥	𝄽	1	2 →	1 + or + 2 or 2 + or + 3 etc.
♪ or 𝅘𝅥𝅮	𝄾	1/2	1 →	1 or + or 2 or + or 3 etc.

Note: "+" is pronounced "and".

This rhythm level chart is very easily adapted to any time signature with **4** as its bottom number. Use it for **2/4** , **3/4** , **4/4** and **6/4** . (In **6/4** time an additional note and rest are used: 𝅝· = six beats; ▬· = six beats.)

Here is an example of counting at the eighth level:

Now, let's bring sixteenth notes (♪ , ♫) and sixteenth rests (𝄿) into the quagmire. A sixteenth of a measure is 1/4 beat, so each sixteenth note or sixteenth rest will get 1/4 beat.

Notice we are not dealing with either the quarter level or the eighth level when quarter beats are being used. Instead, we are now at the sixteenth level.

SIXTEENTH LEVEL RHYTHM CHART

For notes and rests that are divisible by one sixteenth of the measure (1/4 beat).

Type Of Note	Type Of Rest	Number Of Beats	Number Of Symbols Written	Actual Counting Written In Is: (Depending on which beat of the measure the note or rest enters)
𝅝	𝄻	4	16	→ 1 e + a 2 e + a 3 e + a 4 e + a
𝅗𝅥.	𝄼.	3	12	→ 1e+a2e+a3e+a or 2e+a3e+a4e+a
𝅗𝅥	𝄼	2	8	→ 1e+a2e+a or 2e+a3e+a or 3e+a4e+a
𝅘𝅥.	𝄽.	1 1/2	6	→ 1e+a2e or +a2e+a or 2e+a3e etc.
𝅘𝅥	𝄽	1	4	→ 1e+a or +a2e or 2e+a or +a3e etc.
𝅘𝅥𝅮. or 𝅘𝅥𝅯.	𝄾.	3/4	3	→ 1e+ or e+a or 2e+ etc.
𝅘𝅥𝅮 or 𝅘𝅥𝅯	𝄾	1/2	2	→ 1e or e+ or +a or 2e etc.
𝅘𝅥𝅯 or 𝅘𝅥𝅰	𝄿	1/4	1	→ 1 or e or + or a or 2 or e etc.

Note: "e" is pronounced "ē"
        "+" is pronounced "and"
        "a" is pronounced "ă"

This rhythm level chart is very easily adapted to any time signature with **4** as its bottom number. Use it for **2/4** , **3/4** , **4/4** and **6/4** . (In **6/4** time an additional note and rest are used: 𝅝· = six beats; 𝄻· = six beats.) Note: **5/4** time does occur rarely, usually in the jazz idiom.

Here is an example of counting at the sixteenth level:

(Note: 32nd notes and 64th notes do exist, but rarely occur. Two 32nd notes (♫) use the same amount of time as one 16th note and are counted at the 16th level. Four 64th notes (♫♫) use the same amount of time as one 16th note and are counted at the 16th level.)

RHYTHM CHART FOR COUNTING THE TIME SIGNATURE OF $\frac{6}{8}$

The number 6 tells you there are six beats per measure. The number 8 tells you an eighth note will get one beat.

Type Of Note	Type Of Rest	Number Of Beats	Number Of Symbols Written	Actual Counting Written In Is: (Depending on which beat of the measure the note or rest enters)
♩.	▬	6	6 →	1 2 3 4 5 6
♩.	𝄽·	3	3 →	1 2 3 or 4 5 6
♩	𝄽	2	2 →	1 2 or 2 3 etc.
♪ or ♪	𝄾	1	1 →	1 or 2 or 3 etc.

This rhythm level chart is very easily adapted to any time signature with 8 as its bottom number. Use it for $\frac{3}{8}$, $\frac{6}{8}$, $\frac{9}{8}$ and $\frac{12}{8}$. Note: $\frac{5}{8}$ and $\frac{7}{8}$ do occur rarely, usually in the jazz idiom.

How do you know which rhythm chart to use when writing in the counting? Simple! First, notice the time signature. Then look through the song. If you see only the notes and rests found in the quarter level, use the quarter level. If you see notes and rests found in the eighth level, use the eighth level. If you see notes and rests found only in the sixteenth level, use the sixteenth level. If the bottom number of the time signature is an 8 , use the rhythm chart for counting the time signature of $\frac{6}{8}$.

Counting should be written in neatly in line (vertically) with corresponding notes. This makes it very easy to use when counting out loud.

Saying the counting out loud, while playing the notes hands separate, is how you will quickly learn the rhythm of each hand. With the exceptions of triplets and "swing", each symbol must get exactly the same amount of time as all the other symbols. Doing this will result in a desirable steady beat. At least whisper the counting. Don't count in your mind (think the counting without saying it) because you will rationalize and the rhythm won't be there. You will eventually be able to look at a rhythm and know what it sounds like. You will pre-hear the rhythm just before you play it. Until you get to that level of rhythm-reading ability, play it safe: **COUNT OUT LOUD!**

Counting out loud while playing notes is probably the hardest thing you will ever do while learning to play the piano. To make it easier for yourself, understand that most people's natural tendency is to go too fast, too soon, when counting out loud. If you become frustrated, count twice as slowly. If you still become frustrated, slow it down even more! After you have found the speed at which you are able to count out loud while playing, then gradually add speed. A metronome will allow you to add extremely small amounts of speed, so you might consider using one. To go faster, you must intensify your concentration: you are processing the same number of notes in a smaller amount of time. If you go too fast, too soon, your concentration mechanism will revolt. The result is always the same: frustration. So be patient! Increase speed very gradually!

If your best efforts to count out loud still result in frustration, use "pencil tapping" to help yourself out of the rhythmic quagmire. Set your music on a flat surface and, while counting out loud, use the pencil like a drum stick, tapping the pencil's eraser end whenever right hand notes are to be played:

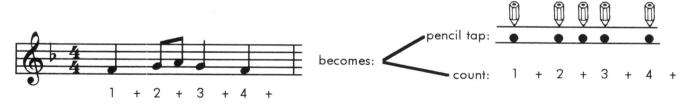

Do the same for the left hand before returning to the piano.
(Note: pencil tapping allows a student to get both the sound and the "feel" of the rhythm without having to concern himself with notes or fingers.)

Lastly, to be certain your rhythm work is correct, record yourself, play it back and listen for rhythmic accuracy.

4.) <u>Hands Together</u> – <u>Learn the notes</u>. Now your coasting into the finish line! Simply go through the song, lining up the notes in both hands. Using the note patterns you learned hands separate will make it much easier to read two or more notes at one time.

5.) <u>Hands Together</u> – <u>Learn the fingers</u>. Make sure the fingering you chose while working hands separate has not changed as a result of putting the song hands together. Also, check the phrasing again.

6.) <u>Hands Together</u> – <u>Learn the rhythm</u>. Remember to work only the rhythm. Make an agreement with yourself, before you start counting out loud, hands together, that you will not stop for wrong notes or fingers. This agreement is more easily kept if you will count very slowly. Give your thinking apparatus a chance to anticipate notes, fingers and rhythm. Learn to crawl before you walk. Learn to walk before you run. Add speed very gradually.

To obtain fluency, you must become capable of looking ahead. You know that when you read words aloud fluently, your eyes and mind stay at least one or two words ahead of your mouth. Likewise, to read notes fluently, your eyes and mind must stay at least one note ahead of your fingers. Until you develop the ability to look ahead, you will be like a driver who, while operating a moving vehicle, opens his car door and looks down at the pavement to see where he is at. This driving stance guarantees accidents...at any speed! The only way to safely move forward is to look ahead! Likewise, staring at a note, while you are playing it, guarantees rhythmic "accidents". You must be continually feeding notes into the cycle: in your eyes, through your mind, out your fingers.

Beginning pianists are "note-o-holics". Even though the wrong note doesn't sound good to the performer, it is amazing how many wrong notes go completely unnoticed by listeners. What listeners easily notice and hate to hear is the interruption of the steady beat. Listeners are "rhythm-o-holics".

Any wrong note you play will remain a little mistake if you maintain the steady beat. Any wrong note you play will become a big mistake if you interrupt the steady beat to go back for the right note. Why make a rhythm mistake out of a note mistake? Why make a big mistake out of a little one? Settle for the little mistake. It's a great habit to cultivate. You will perform the way you practice. Practice maintaining a steady beat!

After all this talk about maintaining a steady beat, you will still be tempted to turn the single mistake of a wrong note into the double mistake of a wrong note and a wrong rhythm. Just know this: Later in this book, I will explain how to completely hide wrong notes through a process known as "resolution". However, I can show you no such trick for hiding the fifth beat of a four-beat measure.

7.) <u>Practice problem spots in small sections</u>. When you hear yourself saying, "I always mess that spot up!" or, "I never can do that spot!", you are ready for section-work. After working a page or two, several times through, counting out loud, there will be certain places in the music that will stand out as "always" or "never" spots. Start one measure before the problem spot and work through it several times, always stopping one measure beyond the problem spot. This means you will be working two, three or four measures, over and over, as many times as is necessary to fix the wrong notes, wrong fingers or wrong rhythm. This is how you will "iron out" all those places where you wanted to stop when you were working the rhythm.

After you have done the section-work, start at the top of the page and maintain a steady beat through the entire page. You will then see the result of your section-work. Quite often, section-work must be repeated over several days of practice before the problem spot is permanently fixed.

If you don't do section-work on problem spots, you will actually be practicing your mistakes. So don't wait to practice in sections. (No need to wonder why the first several measures of a song are so easily performed — they naturally get practiced as a section!)

8.) <u>Add shading</u>. Now that you can mechanically play the notes, fingers and rhythm of a song, let's add the human element: shading. Basically, shading is considered the "faster" (accelerando), "slower" (ritard), "louder" (crescendo) and "softer" (decrescendo) in a piece of music. However, shading also includes style and phrasing.

The term "style" usually refers to the way the composer wants his music performed: mysteriously, or gracefully, or fast, or with tender emotion, etc. However, style also refers to the way the performer chooses to interpret the music at hand. Style markings, when written, are usually found in the upper left corner of a page of music.

The term "phrasing" usually refers to the division of a melody into segments of incomplete musical thought. However, phrasing may also refer to harmony notes as well. A phrase in music is comparable to a phrase in spoken language. Phrases in written music are indicated with slurs, just as phrases in written language are indicated with commas, semicolons or periods.

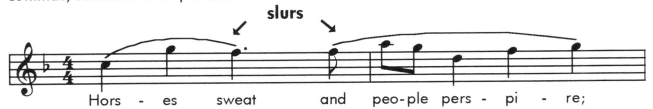

Hors - es sweat and peo-ple pers - pi - re;

eith - er way, they both ti - re.

A slur tells you to play all the notes within a phrase in a smooth and connected manner. (Note: a slur joins either different notes or multiple notes and is not to be confused with a "tie", which joins like notes. A tie tells you to strike the first note once and hold it for the value of both notes.)

Shading allows you, the performer, to interpret music; to inject your personality into what you are playing. Shading is sometimes marked in the music. Like the fingering, what is marked is the composer's or the arranger's suggestion of how he thinks the music should be interpreted. Use what is marked, or feel free to change it to your liking.

Adding the shading to a song is the mark of an experienced performer; one who is no longer just concerned with the mechanical aspects of playing the right notes with the correct fingers and a steady beat. This performer is completely in control, creating the music as he wants it to sound. A listener is immediately attracted to this performer's rhythmic and dynamic contrast, in much the same way that a listener is attracted to a disc jockey's voice more than the voice of someone who speaks in a monotone.

It may seem ironic that the first thing we do after developing the ability to maintain a perfectly steady beat, is speed up certain passages and slow down others. However, what is really happening is just the next logical step: the performer displaying total control over the music, with the listener completely at the effect of the performer's interpretive powers.

Don't be afraid to "bare your soul" when shading music. Exaggerated shading is effective. Make your louds **LOUD!** Make your softs *soft*. However, unless the music calls for sudden changes in volume or speed, taper your shading. Get gradually, yet forcefully louder or softer, faster or slower.

These eight steps are the "how" of practice. Use them and you will be a highly efficient, effective and awesome practicing machine. If you leave out even one step when working on a piece of music that you find challenging, you are taking a big risk.

THE PEDALS

As you approach the intermediate level, you will begin to use the damper pedal.

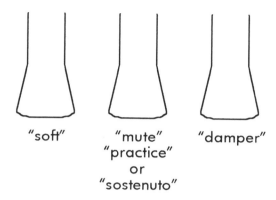

"soft"   "mute"   "damper"
"practice"
or
"sostenuto"

The damper pedal sustains notes by preventing pieces of felt, called "dampers", from dropping back on the strings when you release keys. It is commonly used to connect melody notes and chords which cannot be connected by your fingers. To obtain good connection, you must, in one continuous action, lift the pedal up and push it back down, just after a note or chord is played. When you lift up the pedal, all the notes, except those being held down by your fingers, will be erased. When you push the pedal back down, all the notes being held down by the fingers will be sustained by the pedal. It is the damper pedal's sustaining action which allows your fingers to move on to the next note or notes without losing the sound of previously struck notes.

Use of the damper pedal is indicated in written music one of three ways:

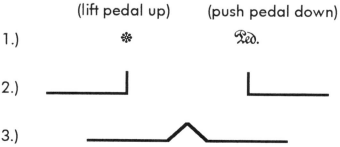

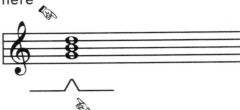

Correct use of the damper pedal
dictates that when the chord is
struck here

the pedal is quickly lifted up
and immediately pushed
back down here.

Then the fingers are free to release the keys and move on to the next note or notes.

Using the damper pedal always feels awkward at first. Usually, within three to six weeks of regular use, you will be capable of using the damper pedal without conscious thought.

The other two pedals are used much less often. The soft pedal lowers the volume and changes the tone quality of the piano. In upright, studio, console and spinet pianos it moves the hammers closer to the strings so that they strike with less momentum. In grand pianos it shifts the entire keyboard to the right just enough so that the mid-range and treble hammers strike one or two strings, instead of three, and the bass hammers strike on their edge, where the felt is not packed down.

The mute, practice or sostenuto pedal varies on different pianos. A mute pedal (also called a "practice pedal") makes use of a piece of felt which drops between the hammers and the strings, creating an extremely soft, harp-like sound. A sostenuto pedal is usually found only on high quality grand pianos. It sustains all the bass keys that are down at the time the pedal is depressed. The damper pedal must be up when the sostenuto pedal is pushed down, though it may be used at will after the sostenuto pedal is down. This makes it possible to sustain an important bass note through passages in the upper voices which requires a change of the damper pedal.

It is important to note that when using the pedal, the piano bench should be positioned far enough away from the piano to allow your heel to remain on the floor. The ball of your foot is used to raise and lower the pedal.

SYMBOLS AND TERMS

<u>Symbol Or Term</u>	<u>Meaning</u>
A Tempo	on time
Accellerando	gradually faster
> (Accent Mark)	strike the note with more force than usual
∧ (Strong Accent)	strike the note with much more force than usual
Ad Lib (Ad Libitum)	"at liberty" - improvise the melody, harmony or rhythm
Adagio	slow
Allegretto	cheerful (fairly fast)
Allegro	fast
Andante	"walking" - casually
Cantabile	in a melodious, singing manner
⊕ (Coda Sign)	"tail" - the ending portion of a song
Con Brio	with vigor and spirit
¢ (Cut Time)	a time signature which indicates to play twice as fast as is written
Crescendo	gradually louder
// (Cut)	cease playing momentarily
D.C.(Da Capo)	return to the beginning
D.C. Al Fine	return to the beginning and play until the "Fine" indication
D.S.(Dal Segno)	return to the sign: 𝄋
D.S. Al Coda	return to the sign and play until the "To Coda" indication, at which time, you will go to the coda
Decrescendo	gradually softer
Diminuendo	gradually softer

▦ (Double Bar)	end of the song
8va - - - - - - - - - ⌐	play eight notes higher than written
8vb - - - - - - - - - ⌐	play eight notes lower than written
Fine	the end
⌐.1.‾‾‾‾‾‾⌐ (First Ending)	play this ending the first time through
f (Forte)	loud
ff (Fortissimo)	extremely loud
Grave	extremely slow (serious manner)
Grazioso	gracefully, elegantly
⌒ (Hold, Bird's Eye or Fermata)	hold note longer than its time value
Largo	very slow (dignified manner)
L.H. (Left Hand)	to be played by the left hand
Legato	long, smooth and connected
Lento	slow
Marcato	play with emphasis (pronounced)
Meno	less
mf (Mezzo-Forte)	moderately loud
mp (Mezzo-Piano)	moderately soft
Moderato	moderate tempo (not too fast)
p (Piano)	soft
pp (Pianissimo)	very soft
Poco A Poco	little by little
Presto	extremely fast
▦ (Repeat Sign)	repeat
R.H. (Right Hand)	to be played by the right hand
Ritard	gradually slower
Scherzando	in a joking, playful manner
⌐.2.‾‾‾‾‾‾⌐ (Second Ending)	play this ending the second time through
𝄋 (Segno)	the sign
Sempre	always
sfz (Sforzando)	"forcing" - sharp, strong accent
Simile	"same" - same as indicated previously
‒ (Slight Accent)	sustain
Staccato	short, detached
Tempo	rate of speed
To Next Strain	skip over the subsequent delineated measures
Vivace	brisk, lively manner

PRACTICE HINTS

-☆- The best times to practice are: 1.) right after lesson, 2.) soon after school or work, and 3.) as early as possible on Saturday and Sunday.

-☆- It's usually better to spend two twenty or thirty minute practice sessions daily than one forty or sixty minute session. Not only does this minimize frustration, it also helps your subconscious absorb the study material.

-☆- Goal-oriented practice is preferable to time-oriented practice. Time-oriented practice is preferable to no practice at all.

-☆- Quality practice requires intense concentration and relaxed finger muscles. When you allow your finger muscles to become tense, your practice and playing will sound forced. So, relax your muscles, but not your focused attention.

-☆- When working a song hands together, many people find it helpful to periodically review it hands separately.

-☆- Use a metronome to help you: 1.) maintain a steady beat, and 2.) gradually add speed. Do not use a metronome until you know the notes and fingers <u>very well</u>. The numbers on the face of a metronome tell you the number of times the metronome will "click" in one minute. (Set the metronome on 60 and a "click" will occur each second.) It is much better to set the metronome on a low number and then gradually add speed, than to set the metronome on a high number and proceed to quickly get frustrated.

-☆- Record yourself playing a piece of music you have practiced. Listen to it as if you were listening to a radio. Then listen to it again, following along in the written music. (Do not play along with the recording.) Mark hesitations. Put brackets around sections that need work. Circle wrong notes, rhythms, etc. After more practice, record yourself again.

-☆- If you decide to change the notes, fingers or rhythm of a song, do so only after successfully practicing and playing what is written. In this way, you are certain to operate out of choice, not necessity.

-☆- Persist.

-☆- Enjoy!

A SPECIAL NOTE TO PARENTS OF PIANO STUDENTS

When your child begins his or her study of piano, you become an important part of a learning triangle. Whether your influence is positive, neutral or negative, you will have a profound effect on your child's learning endeavor. Your active participation will definitely enhance the learning process. Your indifferent attitude will definitely detract from the learning process. Poor communication will discourage learning.

As a piano teacher, I am responsible for, among other things, creating an ideal learning atmosphere in the lesson. As a parent, you are responsible for, among other things, creating an ideal learning atmosphere in the home. To help you understand some of what it takes to create a great learning environment, I have prepared a question and answer session. The following questions are quite common. Of course, my answers vary with each individual situation. However, the answers I have written here are my usual response.

QUESTION: "Why won't my child practice?"
ANSWER: "Because he doesn't want to."

QUESTION: "When my child won't practice, should I force him to practice?"
ANSWER: "To answer your question, I need to know this: Did your child ask for piano lessons or did you decide for him? Also, what's your child's daily schedule?

If your child asked for piano lessons but won't practice, you should provide force as you deem necessary. Until a child develops his own strength of character, he should have access to yours. He came to you wanting lessons. When he got some, he discovered that, while playing the piano is fun, practicing the piano isn't always fun. The problem: He wants to play, but he doesn't want to practice. In this situation, your child is asking to borrow some of your backbone. Give it to him. Though you can't push a rope, you can pull like crazy! See to it that your child follows through on his decision — one or two years of lessons — enough time for him to make an intelligent, informed decision to quit or continue.

If your child did not ask for piano lessons, the answer is not as easy. You, the parents, need to decide whether piano lessons are primarily something you are giving your child or primarily something your child is giving you. If the former is the case, "pull the rope" for as long as you deem appropriate or necessary. If the latter is the case, I recommend stopping lessons and allowing the child to proceed in the directions that his interests lie.

If your child's daily schedule doesn't allow for at least an hour or two of goof-off time, some extra-curricular activities should be cut. Piano may or may not be high on the priority list."

QUESTION: "How can I avoid the almost daily arguments I have with my child about practicing the piano."
ANSWER: "Arguments revolve around reasoning. Reasoning is not a necessary part of good communication. On the contrary, it is often an integral part of poor communication. You may express your intentions, have your child express his intentions and discuss ideas, but do not attempt to reason with your child. Children are experts at their own form of logic. Without reasoning, there is no argument. Without an argument, there is plenty of time left to practice the piano."

QUESTION: "I want to help my child with his daily practice, but his musical knowledge surpassed mine a long time ago. Any suggestions?"
ANSWER: "Yes! Sit in on your child's piano lesson as often as possible. This not only demonstrates caring, it facilitates three-way communication. You will learn the things to listen for in your child's practice.

When possible, stay within earshot of your child's daily practice sessions.

Develop a nurturing attitude. Whenever possible, avoid criticism. Encourage any positive attempts, no matter how small. Promote a feeling of "we're in this together". After all...you are."

CHAPTER THREE
BEGINNER THEORY

There are three main parts to music, as we know it: melody, harmony and rhythm.

INTERVALS

Melody is made up of intervals. When a musician plays an interval and then plays another one behind it, and so on, he is forming a melody. What is an interval? The <u>distance</u> <u>between</u> <u>notes</u>. When measuring intervals, musicians include the notes being struck. So C to D is an interval called a "second"; C to E is an interval called a "third"; and so on, up to an "eighth". (The interval of an eighth is often referred to as an "octave".)

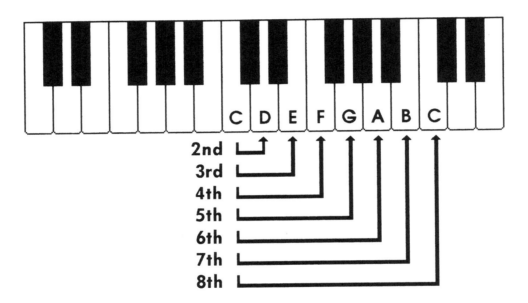

Quite obviously, an interval is exactly two notes: the one you are coming from and the one you are going to. Not so obviously, an interval should be played one note at a time.

CHORDS

Harmony is made up of chords. When a musician plays a chord and then plays another one behind it, and so on, he is forming a harmony. What is a chord? <u>Three or more notes played simultaneously</u>. Two notes played simultaneously imply a chord and are not a chord.

Chords are like people: they're known by the company they keep; and you can't tell very much about them by the way they look. We'll talk later about the company they keep. Let's talk about the way the look. Any chord can be virtually any combination of white and black notes. So, merely looking for certain color combinations will not help you determine any of the various types of chords.

There are four basic chord types: major, minor, diminished and augmented. The major chord is formed by selecting any note, skipping the next <u>three</u> notes to the right (whether black or white), striking the second note, skipping the next <u>two</u> notes to the right (whether black or white) and finally, striking the third note. Congratulations! You have just formed your first chord — illegally! Remember: I said chords are made up of notes played simultaneously. Now form a correct major chord by smacking all three notes down at the same time, being sure to use only the first, third and fifth fingers of either hand.

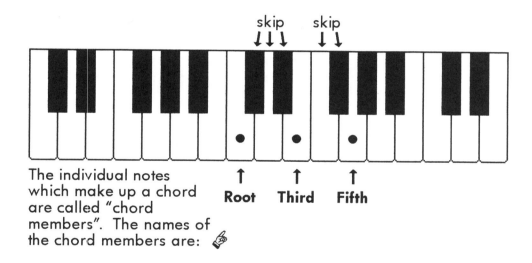

The individual notes which make up a chord are called "chord members". The names of the chord members are:

Root **Third** **Fifth**

We call this chord a "C major chord", simply because we started on the note C. Isn't that exciting?

As you can see, chord members get their names from their relationship to the scale: the root of the C chord is the same as the first note of the C scale; the third of the C chord is the same as the third note of the C scale; the fifth of the C chord is the same as the fifth note of the C scale.

The recipe which is used to form all major chords is very simple: skip three notes, then skip two notes. Let's form a D major chord by starting on the note D and following the recipe:

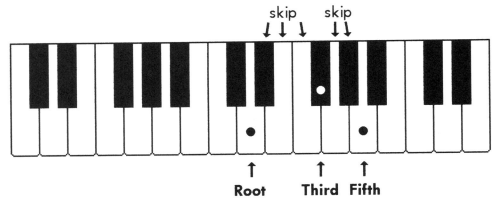

Notice that even though we used the same chord recipe, the third is black.

Here's the B major chord:

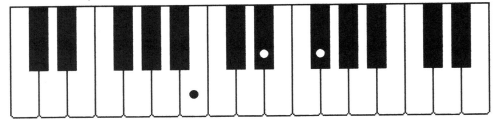

The Ab major chord is an Oreo cookie:

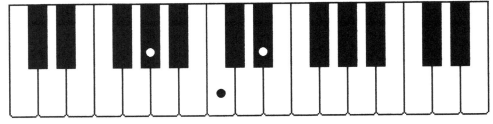

The F# major chord is a "black is beautiful" chord:

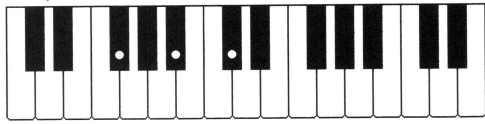

The minor chord is formed by skipping <u>two</u> notes, then skipping <u>three</u> notes. Here's the C minor chord:

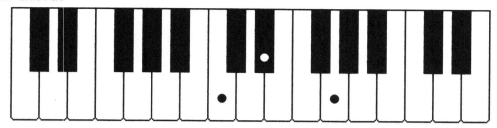

The diminished chord is formed by skipping <u>two</u> notes, then skipping <u>two</u> notes. Here's the C diminished chord:

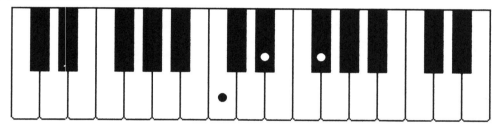

The augmented chord is formed by skipping <u>three</u> notes, then skipping <u>three</u> notes. Here's the C augmented chord:

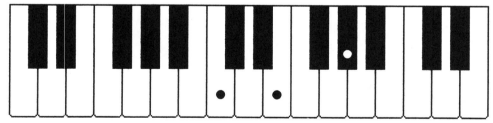

Major, minor, diminished and augmented chords contain three notes, so you will occasionally hear referred to as "triads".

The major chord is called "major" because it's used most often. Remember its recipe as "skip 3, then 2", starting with the bigger number because major connotes big, as in "major league baseball" or a "major disaster".

The minor chord is called "minor" because it's used less often than the major chord. Remember its recipe as "skip 2, then 3", starting with the smaller number because minor connotes small, as in "minor league baseball" or a "minor disaster".

The word "diminish" means "to make smaller", so the diminished chord is made up of the two small numbers: "skip 2, then 2".

The word "augment" means "to make larger", so the augmented chord is made up of the two large numbers: "skip 3, then 3".

Learn to form these chords quickly and easily, using only the first, third and fifth fingers of either hand. A good way to go about this task is to choose a different note, each practice session, on which to form these four triads. Note: to get from a major chord to a minor chord, all you have to do is lower the middle note a half step. This reverses "skip 3, then 2" to "skip 2, then 3". Now you're starting to think like a musician! (Just don't start dressing like us.)

<hr>

RHYTHM

Rhythm is the manipulation of beats and portions of beats. As such, it functions as the vehicle that melody and harmony use to move forward.

To understand rhythm, as it is written in music, you must first understand measures, time signatures, note names, note values, rest names, rest values and rhythm levels. All of these are explained in the third step of the basic practice techniques, found in the second chapter of this book. If you don't already understand these items, may I recommend <u>now</u> as the perfect time to learn them. Have fun!

CHAPTER FOUR
BEGINNER EAR

To play by ear, you must train the contents of the holes on either side of your head. We call this "ear training".

INTERVALS

Begin your ear training by learning to hear the difference among the seven intervals found on page 35. Each interval has its own unique sounds:

2nd - sounds like the beginning of a scale (do, re)
3rd - sounds like a doorbell (play it backwards)
4th - sounds like "Here Comes The Bride" or "O Christmas Tree"
5th - sounds like "Star Wars" or "Chariots Of Fire"
6th - sounds like "America" or "My Bonnie" or "NBC Theme"
7th - sounds like car horns blaring in traffic
8th - sounds like "Over The Rainbow"

Play these and listen to them. To get to the point where you are able to consistently hear the difference among them, you will have to get someone else to play them for you. This will allow you to sit across the room, look the other way and identify each interval solely by sound. Your assistant can be anyone intelligent enough to mix the intervals up in random fashion. Most piano teachers qualify for this task.

When you are able to aurally identify each randomly-played interval (eight out of ten is okay for starters), move on to the four triads.

CHORDS

Learning to hear the difference among the four triads is much more difficult than learning to hear the difference among the seven intervals because you are hearing three notes sounding simultaneously. Each note confounds the others.

The easiest way to learn to aurally distinguish among the four triads is to listen for the overall sound quality. Major sounds happy. Minor sounds sad. Learn to hear the difference between these two by having an assistant play them on different notes, randomly. Then add the diminished and augmented chords.

Diminished sounds "made smaller" or "crunched up". Augmented sounds "made larger" or "spread out". Listening to hear whether the fifth is lowered (as in the diminished chord) or raised (as in the augmented chord) is a help to some people. Your assistant can be anyone competent enough to play the four triads in random fashion. Again, most piano teachers qualify for this task.

When you are able to aurally identify each randomly-played chord (eight out of ten is okay for starters), you are done! That's all there is to beginning ear training. I'll bet you thought I couldn't write a chapter this short.

CHAPTER FIVE
INTERMEDIATE PERFORMANCE

WHAT TO PRACTICE

Any good teacher is capable of teaching you what he wants you to know, through music of your choosing. Any good teacher realizes the important part <u>desire</u> plays in learning. The old saying goes: "You can lead a horse to water, but you can't make him drink." Well, if you add plenty of salt to a horse's oats, not only will he drink, he'll lead <u>you</u> to water. Your being allowed to choose the music you work on is any good teacher's way of "salting your oats".

I heartily recommend choosing any music that appeals to you, from the <u>Michael Aaron Piano Course</u> (Grade Three and Grade Four), published by Belwin Mills. These two books contain well known, intermediate level classical music. Another excellent, intermediate level classical book is <u>Music By The Masters</u>, compiled, edited and annotated by Russell E. Lanning, published by Musicord Publications (a division of Belwin Mills). If you prefer more variety, you may opt to learn music from <u>Teacher's Choice For The Young Pianist</u> (Early Grade), arranged by Allan Small, published by Alfred Publishing Company. In addition, I recommend choosing several popular song books that appeal to you. Sheet music is yet another possibility, if you don't mind the expense. For intermediate level technical exercises, I recommend <u>A Dozen A Day</u> (Book Two and Book Three), published by Willis Music Company.

THE DIVIDED LINE

At the intermediate level, in both your classical and popular music, you will notice a new phenomenon: the divided line. Here is an example:

The quarter rest, on the first beat, is telling you to be quiet. The note D, on the first beat, is telling you to make noise. How can you do both? By realizing you have two separate lines of music, on the same staff, being played simultaneously, by one hand.

The top line looks like this:

The bottom line looks like this:

The divided line is truly misnamed. It should have been called a "united line", because the composer took two separate lines of music and united them (i.e. crammed them together) on one staff. Nevertheless, we musicians have chosen to call this a divided line, probably because it's up to us, as performers, to divide the lines in our thinking, while uniting the lines in our performance.

The trick to reading divided lines is quite simple: read vertically. In the example, while playing the note D on beat one, notice the quarter rest above it, which is telling you to bring the F# in on beat two. Likewise, in the second measure, the top note A is held down for two beats, while the quarter note D (beat one) goes to the quarter note E (beat two). As long as you line up each note and/or rest with its corresponding beat, no problems will result.

At the intermediate level, you will also be called upon to handle two new types of rhythm: "dotted eighth sixteenths" and "triplets".

DOTTED EIGHTH SIXTEENTHS

A dotted eighth note followed by a sixteenth note is referred to as a "dotted eighth sixteenth" (♪. ♬). In classical music, dotted eighth sixteenths are counted and performed very precisely. The dotted eighth note gets exactly three fourths of a beat (counted "1 e +") and the sixteenth note gets exactly one fourth of a beat (counted "a"). In popular music, dotted eighth sixteenths are counted and performed more loosely. The dotted eighth note gets two thirds of a beat (counted "1 da") and the sixteenths note gets one third of a beat (counted "da").

Classical   Popular

  1 e + a   1 da da

When popular musicians count dotted eighth sixteenths, they usually allow time for the first "da" without actually saying it. The result is:

1   da 2   da 3   da 4   da

This is known as "swing" or "swinging it". When eighth notes are counted this same way, it is also referred to as "swing" or "swinging it":

1 da 2 da 3 da 4 da

TRIPLETS

A "triplet" is any of the following:

- three notes of equal value, occurring within 1/2 of a beat:

- three notes of equal value, occurring within one beat:

- three notes of equal value, evenly spread over two beats:

- three notes of equal value, evenly spread over four beats:

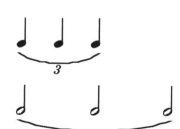

Eighth note triplet are counted:

1 da da

Each note gets exactly one third of a beat.

Quarter note triplets are counted:

1 da da 2 da da

Each note gets exactly two thirds of a beat.

Half note triplets are counted:

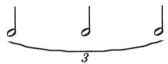

1 da da 2 da da 3 da da 4 da da

Each note gets exactly one and one third beats.

Eighth note triplets and quarter note triplets are quite common, while half note triplets occur so rarely, you might live long enough to see them once or twice in written music. Sixteenth note triplets are also very rare. They are counted:

+ e a   or   1 e a

Each note gets one sixth of a beat. For example:

1   +ea   2ea   +

TWO HAND METHOD

Two Hand Method is the beginning point of chord symbol performance. When you play this way, you have two separate ideas going on simultaneously:

        1.) your right hand, playing the melody

        2.) your left hand, playing the harmony

The result is no surprise: it sounds like two hands are playing the piano.

Your right hand will play the melody exactly as it is written. In music with one treble clef and no bass clef (called "lead sheets" or "fake sheets"), the melody will be the notes that are written:

In music with one treble clef and one bass clef, the melody will always be the highest note in the treble clef:

Your right hand will play <u>only</u> the melody notes. Ignore all notes written under the melody, whether in treble or bass clef.

In music with two treble clefs and one bass clef, the melody will always be found in the top treble clef:

Again, your right hand will play only the melody notes. Ignore all notes written under the melody, whether in treble or bass clef. (The notes written on the two bottom staves are used by musicians who are able to play only by note, or by musicians who opt to play the music by note, instead of by chord symbol.)

Your left hand will play the chord symbols. They are found just above each line of music. In the preceding examples, the letters "F" and "C" are chord symbols. (If you are unsure how to form chords on the piano keyboard, review the section of chapter three devoted to this topic.)

When a composer or arranger wants you to play a major chord, he will write a single letter. This letter tells your left hand which note to start on, when forming the chord on the piano. So, when the letter "C" is printed above the music, your left hand will play a C major chord. Your hand will strike the chord on the beat that lines up with the chord symbol, and hold it down until the next chord symbol, at which time your hand will strike the next chord, and so on.

When a composer or arranger wants you to play a minor chord, he will write a letter and put either a small letter "m" or a "–" beside it. So, when "Cm" or "C–" is printed above the music, your left hand will play a C minor chord.

When a composer or arranger wants you to play a diminished chord, he will write a letter and put either a "°" or "dim" beside beside it. So, when "C°" or "C dim" is printed above the music, your left hand will play a C diminished chord.

When a composer or arranger wants you to play an augmented chord, he will write a letter and put either a "+", "(#5)" or "aug" beside it. So, when "C+", "C(#5)" or "C aug" is printed above the music, your left hand will play a C augmented chord.

Don't be surprised if the music you are playing doesn't contain any diminished or augmented chords. In most music, diminished and augmented chords are used sparingly.

Ignore any portion of the chord symbol that I have not explained to you yet. In other words, if you see "F sus", play an F major chord and ignore the "sus".
If you see "C maj7(#5)", play a C(#5) chord and ignore the "maj7". Simple!?!

Follow the "Basic Practice Techniques", just as you do when learning to play by note. Be certain your left hand is using only the first, third and fifth fingers when playing the chords. Also, be sure you can get to each chord quickly and easily (no hesitations or pauses), before you begin to practice the music hands together. Once again, a metronome will help you. Set it at 60 and give each chord four "clicks", then three, then two.

When working hands together, keep the left hand chord as close as possible to the right hand melody notes. However, do not allow the left hand chord members to overlap the melody. The melody should always be the highest sounding note.

Also, remember: <u>chord symbols supersede the key signature</u>. For example: the G chord will always contain the notes G, B, and D, even when the key signature contains a Bb.

After you are comfortable playing Two Hand Method this way, turn to chapter six and read the section devoted to chords. For your next trick, learn Two Hand Method using the seven chord recipes and any of the ten common "special instruction" chords which show up in music you are choosing to play. Be patient with yourself. Take your time. Enjoy!

If you have trouble remembering all the notes of certain chords and feel the urge to write down each chord member, do so on a separate piece of paper. Do not write chord members on your music, beside the chord symbol, because you will learn to read what you have written instead of learning to read the chord symbol. By writing the chord symbol, with its chord members, on a separate piece of paper, you are forced to look away from the music to find out what you don't know. In this way, you will learn how to read the chord symbols much more quickly, because looking them up is tedious. Ideally, you would not write down anything, anywhere; instead, choosing to remember the seven chord recipes, while looking up any "special instruction" chords you might run into. The chord explanations I have provided cover the logic behind each chord symbol. Remembering this logic (i.e. the reasoning behind each component part of a chord symbol) is the fastest way to understand and learn to play using the chord symbols.

THREE HAND METHOD

When your Two Hand Method songs are learned quickly and easily, you are ready for Three Hand Method. Three Hand Method is very impressive-sounding. Anyone who listens to you playing Three Hand Method will think you have been studying piano a lot longer than you actually have. (Don't let them in on the secret. Let them think you are exceptionally talented!) When you play Three Hand Method, you have three separate ideas going on simultaneously:

1.) your right hand, playing the melody
2.) your right hand, playing the harmony
3.) your left hand, playing the bass line

The result: it sounds like three hands are playing the piano. Because your right hand is doing the work of two hands, your left hand is able to become the "third hand".

There are four steps to learning Three Hand Method. Follow each step very carefully. The first time through these four steps is always the most difficult. Choose a song you really like, maybe one you already know through Two Hand Method. Make sure this first Two Hand Method song contains no more than eight or ten different chords. Here goes! Step 1. Learn how to play the chord symbols in root position. Root position is the way your left hand played the chord symbols in Two Hand Method. After you can play the root position chords in each hand separately, play the root position chords hands together. Keep your hands as close as possible. For example: When your right hand is playing a C chord, starting on middle C, your left hand should be playing its C chord starting on the next C down, not two or three octaves down. So, when doing root position chords hands together, your hands should never be more than several notes apart. For this step, ignore how long each chord is supposed to be held down. Instead, give each chord the same number of beats. When you can get through the root position chords hands together, with a steady beat (giving each chord either four, three or two beats), you are ready to move on to the next step. Step 2. Learn how to play the chord symbols in inversion form. You will do this step by starting on root position with the first chord, then going to the absolute closest position of the next chord, etc., till all the chords in the song have been played. To go to the absolute closest position of the following chord, you must answer three questions between each chord change:

1.) What notes are in the next chord?
2.) Am I already on any of the next chord's notes?
3.) Which notes are lacking?

For example: Say the first chord of the song you are playing is a C chord and it is going to an F chord, then a G chord, then back to a C chord. Here's what would happen: You would play the C chord in root position. While holding it down, ask yourself the first question. "What notes are in the next chord?" Answer: F, A, C. Then, still holding down the C chord, ask yourself the second question. "Am I already on any of the next chord's notes?" Answer: Yes, C. Then, still holding down the C chord, ask yourself the third question. "Which notes are lacking?" Answer: F, A. Then, while holding the note C down, move the notes E and G to F and A, but don't strike the F and A. Just hold your fingers over the new notes. Release the C. Then strike all three notes in the F chord simultaneously. You have successfully gone from the C chord to the absolute closest position of the F chord.

Here's where you started:

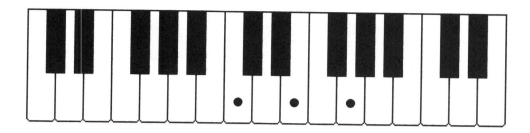

Here's where you ended up:

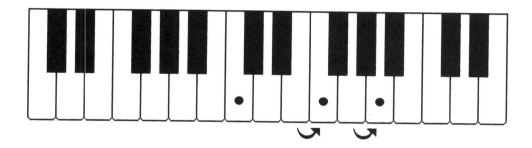

We call this new position of the F chord an "inversion", meaning "turned upside-down". Notice the note C, which was on top of the root position F chord, is now on the bottom of the inverted F chord.

Now let's go to the next chord: G. While holding the inverted F chord down, ask yourself the three questions again. "What notes are in the next chord?" G, B, D. "Am I already on any of the next chord's notes?" No. "Which notes are lacking?" G, B, D. The absolute closest position of the next chord is:

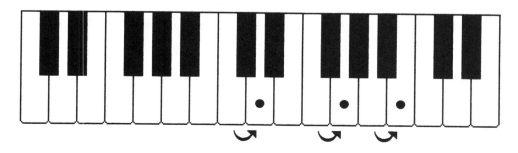

However, this is very close too:

Handle this situation like horse shoes and hand grenades: close counts. It doesn't really matter which position of the G chord you go to. They're both very close.

Now let's go to the next chord: C. While holding down whichever position of the G chord you chose, ask yourself the three questions again. "What notes are in the next chord?" C, E, G. "Am I already on any of the next chord's notes?" Yes, G. "Which notes are lacking?" C, E. Depending on which position of the G chord you chose, the C chord would either look like this:

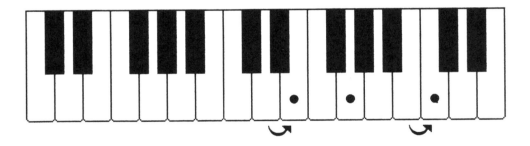

or this:

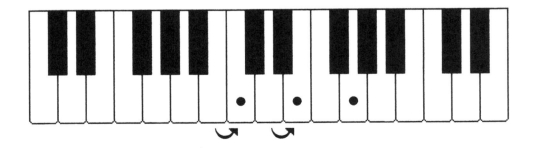

When practicing Step 2. , not every chord will end up in an inverted position. You will occasionally land on a root position chord. However, because most of the chords are played in an inverted position, we call this step "learning how to play chord symbols in inversion form".

Now I'll show you how we label and finger the different chord positions. Three-note chords have three positions:

<u>Root Position</u>

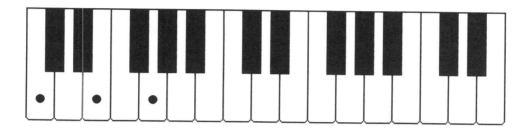

<u>First Inversion</u> (turned upside-down once)

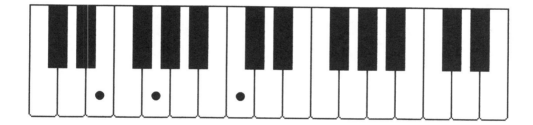

<u>Second Inversion</u> (turned upside-down a second time)

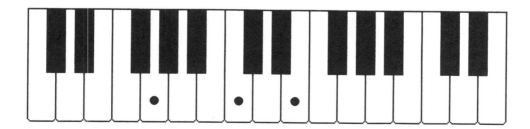

(If we turned this triad upside-down one more time, we would be returning to a root position chord, one octave higher than where we started.)

Four-note chords have four positions:

Root Position

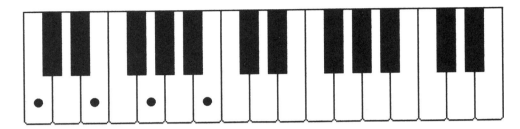

First Inversion

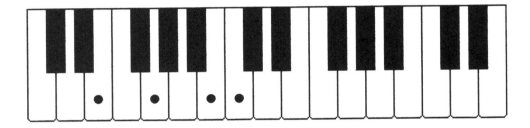

Second Inversion

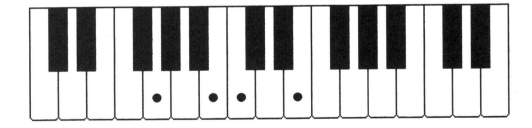

Third Inversion

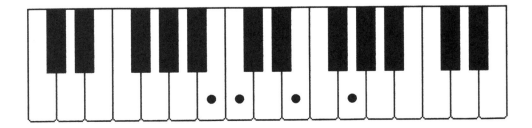

Moving from root position through each inversion, we are just taking the bottom note and placing it on top. Simple!

I wish I could say that learning to finger the various chord positions is easy. It's not. But it is very worthwhile. Learning the correct fingering of each chord position makes the chords much more accessible. Practice the following exercise, hands separate and hands together, till the correct fingering of each chord position is a habit. (You do not have to completely master this exercise before moving on to the third step.)

CHORD POSITION FINGER EXERCISE

Practice going up and down the keyboard, playing solid chords (i.e. all chord members struck simultaneously), using the fingering indicated.

The standard finger pattern for triads:	Left Hand	Right Hand
Root Position:	5 3 1	1 3 5
1st Inversion:	5 3 1	1 2 5
2nd Inversion:	5 2 1	1 3 5

The standard finger pattern for 7th chords:	Left Hand	Right Hand
Root Position:	5 3 2 1	1 2 3 5
1st Inversion:	5 3 2 1	1 2 4 5
2nd Inversion:	5 3 2 1	1 2 3 5
3rd Inversion:	5 4 2 1	1 2 3 5

Now let's get back to the song you are practicing. When you are able to play the inversions in each hand separately, put the inversions hands together. Ignore how long each chord is supposed to be held down. Instead, give each chord the same number of beats. When you can get through the inversions hands together, with a steady beat (giving each chord either four, three or two beats), you are ready to move on to the next step. Step 3. Learn how to play the melody and the harmony, using only your right hand. Leave your left hand in your lap. If any melody notes precede the first chord symbol, play them. When you arrive at the first chord symbol, play the corresponding melody note with all the chord members you are able to simultaneously reach, being sure to keep the melody note above (i.e. to the right of) any and all chord members. Then play the next melody note with all the chord members you are able to simultaneously reach, being sure to keep the melody note above the chord members.

Keep doing this until the next chord symbol, at which time, you will play the new chord members under the melody. Be sure that you are striking full chords with each melody note.

When melody notes are close together, you will be re-striking many of the same notes:

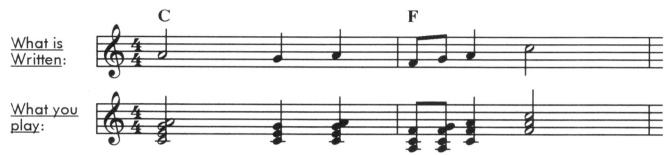

When melody notes are spread out, you will not be re-striking many of the same notes:

Keep in mind: This is the most difficult of the four steps. Your right hand will be doing more than what both hands were doing when you were a "tiny Two Hander". To do this step correctly, you <u>must</u> keep the melody above the chords. This means the melody note will always be the note furthest to your right. Any note you mistakenly place above the melody (i.e. to the right of the melody) will become the "new" melody note, and will be the <u>*wrong*</u> melody note. So, keep all chord members <u>under</u> the melody.

After you are capable of playing full chords with each melody note, go back and streamline this third step by re-striking fewer chords. One reason you are re-striking chords is to disguise the chord changes. You don't want: note, note, note, chord, note, note, note, note, note, chord, note, note, etc. , where the only time you hear a chord, is at a chord change. However, you also don't want: chord, chord, chord, chord, chord, chord, etc. , where you never get to hear the beautiful sound of a single note. What you are looking for is the sound created by re-striking chords, but not with each and every melody note. Chords are meant to complement and support a melody — not blow it away.

So, if you are not going to strike a chord with each melody note, how do you decide which melody notes deserve a chord? The rule is simple: <u>Fast notes don't need full chords</u>. When a sixteenth note or an eighth note demands that you change your hand position, just so you can strike a full chord with it, realize that these notes only sound a very short while. If it's convenient (i.e. you don't have to change your hand position), feel free to strike full chords with these notes. If it's a hassle (i.e. you have to lift your hand from one position and move it to another), feel free to strike partial chords with these notes, or simply play single notes. Keep in mind: While fast notes don't need full chords, slow notes usually do. Half notes, dotted-half notes and whole notes are heard longer, and are usually desirous of something with which to enhance themselves. Full chords "fill the bill" very nicely. Quarter notes are not fast or slow, so, when deciding whether to use full chords, partial chords or single notes, refer to your whim. Remember that the damper pedal is holding full and partial chords through many of your single notes. This observation alone, should help you minimize your hand position changes. Generally, you should have no more than one or two hand position changes per chord change.

Let's look at the examples I showed you, to see how might play them now, minimizing hand position changes and finding a balance among full chords, partial chords and single notes.

Comparing these two examples to the first two, you notice fewer hand position changes, and a pleasant balance among full chords, partial chords and single notes. In a single stroke, we have made this third step both easier to play and more beautiful to hear. Now, that's exciting!

Note: the fourth note of a scale does not create a desirable sound when played simultaneously with the third of the chord. The third is the strongest (i.e. most colorful) chord member. The fourth is one half step up from the third — too close to harmonize with it, and close enough to "grind" with it. For this reason, when the melody note is a fourth (i.e. four notes up from the root of the chord), leave the third out of the right hand chord. This example demonstrates the difference:

Undesirable - third and fourth sounding simultaneously

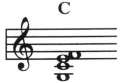

Desirable - fourth sounding without third

Also note: when eighth or sixteenth notes are tied over a bar line, at a chord change, your right hand will strike the new chord early. In the following example, the right hand strikes the G chord on the "+" of beat 4, not on beat one:

When practicing Step 3. , don't attempt to get the fewest possible hand position changes, or the perfect balance among full chords, partial chords and single notes. Close counts, dadgummit! When you don't nit-pik the details, more learning will take place, the process will be more enjoyable, and the end result will be more desirable. Enjoy!

When you've got the notes, fingers and rhythm, move on to the fourth and final step.

<u>Step 4</u>. Learn how to add a bass line. Begin by having your left hand play octaves, obtained from reading the chord symbol. For example: when the chord symbol is "G", your left hand will play two G's simultaneously, using the first and fifth fingers. You will play this "G" octave on the beat which lines up with the chord symbol, and hold it down until the next chord symbol, at which time, you will move to whatever octave the next chord symbol dictates. When you are able to play the left hand octaves through the entire song, combine your right hand (playing Step 3.) with your left hand (playing octaves). This combination will sound very rich and full, but we're not quite finished.

When you have the correct notes, fingers and rhythm, add the fifth in the left hand. Here's how: With your first and fifth fingers holding an octave, press your second finger down. It will naturally fall on the fifth, every time! How convenient! [Note: your left hand will play either the octave <u>or</u> the fifth, not both simultaneously. For example: when the chord symbol is "G", your left hand will play either the "G" octave <u>or</u> the note "D" (the fifth).] Your left hand may either the octave or the fifth, at any time, provided you don't create a predictable pattern. In other words: Do not play octave, fifth, octave, fifth, etc. or octave, octave, fifth, octave, octave, fifth, etc. This quickly tires the listener's ears. (Note: when diminished or augmented chords occur, either leave out the fifth entirely, or modify the fifth to comply with the chord.)

When the fifth becomes comfortable, your left hand may further vary its repertoire by re-striking either the top note or the bottom note of the octave. This will make it much easier to "mix up" the left hand notes, thereby avoiding any predictable pattern. So, at any given moment during the performance of Step 4., your left hand may be playing either the octave, the fifth, the bottom note of the octave or the top note of the octave.

When including the damper pedal with Step 4., note that the fifth may sound with the octave, bottom note or top note, so long as it is not struck simultaneously with the octave, bottom note or top note. If you inadvertently strike the fifth simultaneously with the octave, bottom note or top note, you will notice the undesirable "Indians are coming" sound.

When you have the notes, fingers and rhythm, hands together, you are a full-fledged "Three Hander". After you have learned several songs using Three Hand Method, begin to add "fill" notes by re-striking chord members where you might normally be observing rests or playing held tones (i.e. long-sounding notes). For example:

At any given moment, one of four possibilities prevails:

    1.) both hands are playing notes
    2.) just the right hand is playing notes
    3.) just the left hand is playing notes
    4.) neither hand is playing notes
       (i.e. either the pedal is holding notes
       previously played or silence prevails)

When adding fill notes, you should maintain a balance among these four possibilities. Too much of one, or not enough of another, is undesirable.

Ideally, fill notes should vary, at least slightly, every time you play a song.

Let's summarize Three Hand Method:

Step 1. Root position chords
Step 2. Inversions
Step 3. RH plays melody over chord
Step 4. LH adds bass line

The first step is designed to teach you the chords. The second step forces you to become familiar with individual chord members. These first two steps lay the groundwork for the third step. Initially, it is extremely important that you lay this groundwork because the third step requires you to perform your chords (thinking in terms of) right to left (i.e. from the melody, down), instead of left to right (i.e. locating the root, then the third, then the fifth). When you become familiar with many commonly used chords, the first two steps will become unnecessary. Eventually, the third and fourth steps will also become unnecessary. You will be sight-reading Three Hand Method, reading music as comfortably as you read a newspaper.

If you think Three Hand Method is some kind of musical shorthand cheating, fear not. It is.

ARPEGGIATION METHOD

To understand Arpeggiation Method, you must first understand what it means to arpeggiate a chord. Arpeggiating a chord is simply playing the notes of a chord in rapid, even succession. An arpeggiated chord is called an "arpeggio" (an Italian word meaning "chord as played on a harp") or a "broken chord" (English words meaning "chord in pieces").

Arpeggiation Method is simply Three Hand Method with the addition of arpeggios as fill notes. When they provide a sense of direction, or when they lead back into the song's melody notes, arpeggios will add a pleasant rambling quality to your music. However, if arpeggios are allowed to wander aimlessly, they will add an unpleasant rambling quality to your music.

Here are some examples of Arpeggiation Method:

<u>What is written:</u>

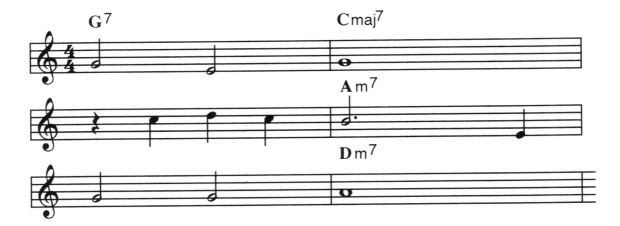

What you might play: (Intermediate Level)

What you might play: (Advanced Level)

Notice that the left hand occasionally makes use of a seventh or a tenth to enhance its "octave and fifth" routine. Also, notice that the left hand is free to leave its "octave and fifth" routine to help out with the arpeggios.

Arpeggiation is a great way to spruce up virtually any melody — especially melodies which contain a lot of held tones. Have fun with it!

SCALES

Music has two main aspects: pitch and duration. "Pitch" refers to highness or lowness of sound. "Duration" refers to the length of time that sound lasts. Both melody and harmony are pitch-related, while rhythm is solely about duration.

Music contains a central pitch around which melody and harmony are written. This central pitch is the nucleus of a collection of pitches used to construct <u>tonal</u> (i.e. pitch-centered) music. (<u>Atonal</u> or <u>pantonal</u> music contains no central pitch, is rare and, to most people's ears, borders on noise.) When a musician is aware of both the central pitch and the surrounding collection of pitches used to construct the music he is writing or performing, he operates at a tremendous advantage over his less knowledgeable counterparts.

When the central pitch and its surrounding collection of pitches are arranged sequentially, in ascending and/or descending order, the result is a scale. Besides being excellent finger exercises, scales are the most efficient devices yet created for orienting students of music to both the central pitch and its surrounding collection of pitches. In other words, scale knowledge is **big-time important!**

There are twelve different notes on the piano, and there's a major and a minor scale for each. Learn one new scale each week, while reviewing the "old" ones, and you will know the scales in twenty four (24) weeks. If scales make your blood run thick, learn one new scale every two (2) weeks, while reviewing the "old" ones. This will get you the scales in one (1) year (including a two week vacation and two weeks "sick leave").

All tonal music is written with some scale in mind. Whether you are a piano hobbyist, piano student or piano professional, knowing the scale "behind" the music you are playing gives you a big advantage. Every fine musician I've ever worked with knows the scales. Pay your dues. Learn the scales. Here they are:

MAJOR SCALES

(Note: when playing scales hands together, the left hand plays one octave lower than the right hand. The finger numbers in parenthesis are to be used for multi-octave scales.)

<u>C Major Scale</u>:

| R.H. | 1 | 2 | 3 | 1 | 2 | 3 | 4 | 5 | | 4 | 3 | 2 | 1 | 3 | 2 | 1 |
| L.H. | 5 | 4 | 3 | 2 | 1 | 3 | 2 | 1 | | 2 | 3 | 1 | 2 | 3 | 4 | 5 |

R.H. (1) above between 5 and 4

L.H. (1) below first note, and (1) below last note

<u>Db Major Scale</u>:

| R.H. | 2 | 3 | 1 | 2 | 3 | 4 | 1 | 2 | | 1 | 4 | 3 | 2 | 1 | 3 | 2 |
| L.H. | 3 | 2 | 1 | 4 | 3 | 2 | 1 | 3 | | 1 | 2 | 3 | 4 | 1 | 2 | 3 |

<u>D Major Scale</u>:

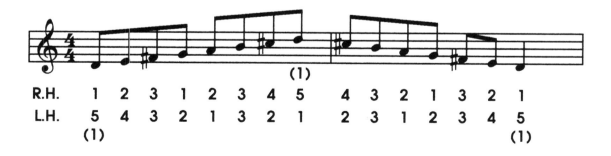

| R.H. | 1 | 2 | 3 | 1 | 2 | 3 | 4 | 5 | | 4 | 3 | 2 | 1 | 3 | 2 | 1 |
| L.H. | 5 | 4 | 3 | 2 | 1 | 3 | 2 | 1 | | 2 | 3 | 1 | 2 | 3 | 4 | 5 |

(1) below R.H. first note, (1) below L.H. last note

Eb Major Scale:

R.H.	3	1	2	3	4	1	2	3		2	1	4	3	2	1	3
L.H.	3	2	1	4	3	2	1	3		1	2	3	4	1	2	3

E Major Scale:

R.H.	1	2	3	1	2	3	4	5		4	3	2	1	3	2	1
L.H.	5	4	3	2	1	3	2	1		2	3	1	2	3	4	5
(1)															(1)

F Major Scale:

R.H.	1	2	3	4	1	2	3	1		3	2	1	4	3	2	1
L.H.	5	4	3	2	1	3	2	1		2	3	1	2	3	4	5
(1)															(1)

Gb Major Scale:

R.H.	2	3	4	1	2	3	1	2		1	3	2	1	4	3	2
L.H.	4	3	2	1	3	2	1	4		1	2	3	1	2	3	4

G Major Scale:

							(1)							
R.H.	1	2	3	1	2	3	4	5	4	3	2	1	3	2	1
L.H.	5	4	3	2	1	3	2	1	2	3	1	2	3	4	5
	(1)													**(1)**

Ab Major Scale:

R.H.	3	4	1	2	3	1	2	3	2	1	3	2	1	4	3
L.H.	3	2	1	4	3	2	1	3	1	2	3	4	1	2	3

A Major Scale:

							(1)							
R.H.	1	2	3	1	2	3	4	5	4	3	2	1	3	2	1
L.H.	5	4	3	2	1	3	2	1	2	3	1	2	3	4	5

Bb Major Scale:

R.H.	4	1	2	3	1	2	3	4	3	2	1	3	2	1	4
L.H.	3	2	1	4	3	2	1	3	1	2	3	4	1	2	3

B Major Scale:

									(1)							
R.H.	1	2	3	1	2	3	4	5	4	3	2	1	3	2	1
L.H.	1	3	2	1	4	3	2	1	2	3	4	1	2	3	1

MINOR SCALES

There are three forms of minor: natural, harmonic and melodic. (See chapter six: "Mutations And The Forms Of Minor".) The following minor scales are written in the natural form.

A Minor Scale:

									(1)							
R.H.	1	2	3	1	2	3	4	5	4	3	2	1	3	2	1
L.H.	5	4	3	2	1	3	2	1	2	3	1	2	3	4	5
	(1)														(1)

Bb Minor Scale:

R.H.	4	1	2	3	1	2	3	4	3	2	1	3	2	1	4
L.H.	2	1	3	2	1	4	3	2	3	4	1	2	3	1	2

B Minor Scale:

R.H.	1	2	3	1	2	3	4	5		4	3	2	1	3	2	1
L.H.	1	3	2	1	4	3	2	1		2	3	4	1	2	3	1

(1)

C Minor Scale:

R.H.	1	2	3	1	2	3	4	5		4	3	2	1	3	2	1
L.H.	5	4	3	2	1	3	2	1		2	3	1	2	3	4	5

(1)   (1)   (1)

C# Minor Scale:

R.H.	3	4	1	2	3	1	2	3		2	1	3	2	1	4	3
L.H.	3	2	1	4	3	2	1	3		1	2	3	4	1	2	3

D Minor Scale:

R.H.	1	2	3	1	2	3	4	5		4	3	2	1	3	2	1
L.H.	5	4	3	2	1	3	2	1		2	3	1	2	3	4	5

(1)   (1)   (1)

Eb Minor Scale:

R.H.	3	1	2	3	4	1	2	3	2	1	4	3	2	1	3
L.H.	2	1	4	3	2	1	3	2	3	1	2	3	4	1	2

E Minor Scale:

R.H.	1	2	3	1	2	3	4	5	4	3	2	1	3	2	1
L.H.	5	4	3	2	1	3	2	1	2	3	1	2	3	4	5
	(1)														(1)

F Minor Scale:

R.H.	1	2	3	4	1	2	3	1	3	2	1	4	3	2	1
L.H.	5	4	3	2	1	3	2	1	2	3	1	2	3	4	5
	(1)														(1)

F# Minor Scale:

R.H.	3	4	1	2	3	1	2	3	2	1	3	2	1	4	3
L.H.	4	3	2	1	3	2	1	4	1	2	3	1	2	3	4

G Minor Scale:

R.H.	1	2	3	1	2	3	4	5	4	3	2	1	3	2	1
								(1)							
L.H.	5	4	3	2	1	3	2	1	2	3	1	2	3	4	5
	(1)														(1)

G# Minor Scale:

R.H.	3	4	1	2	3	1	2	3	2	1	3	2	1	4	3
L.H.	3	2	1	3	2	1	4	3	4	1	2	3	1	2	3

Notice that scale fingerings are designed to keep your thumbs on white notes. This is for both comfort and convenience. When playing scales, black notes are less accessible to your thumbs because: 1.) the thumbs originate further back in your hand than the other fingers, and 2.) the thumbs use their side to strike notes.

Notice that the starting fingers end each scale (with the exception of the fifth finger). This is to allow the musician the freedom of playing two, three or four octave scales, duplicating the same finger pattern in each octave.

Notice that the fourth finger is the only finger to play one note per octave. Generally, when the fourth finger plays its note, all the other fingers will fall in place.

Being able to play the scales with a steady beat, hands together, is all that is necessary to "know" them. However, the faster you are able to play the scales, the more useful they will become. The most efficient way to develop speed on your scales is by building endurance. Here's how:

THE MARATHON SCALE

Choose your favorite scale. Learn to do this scale covering four octaves in each hand (i.e. four octaves up and four octaves down). Then put it hands together, keeping your hands one octave apart.

Set your metronome on 60. (The numbers on the face of a metronome indicate the number of times it "clicks" in one minute, so setting the metronome on 60 will produce one "click" each second.) Play your four octave scale, hands together, placing each successive note of the scale with each successive "click" of the metronome. When 60 is a comfortable speed for you, move the metronome setting to 63. When 63 is a comfortable speed for you, move the metronome setting to 66, and so on, through 69, 72, 76 etc. , all the way up to 208. Take your time, be thorough, and do not skip even one metronome setting.

When 208 is a comfortable speed for you, drop the metronome setting to 104 and play two notes per "click". (This is the same speed you were going when you had the metronome set on 208, playing one note per "click".) You will have to listen much more carefully. To work your way back up to 208, two notes per "click", you will have to build a lot of endurance. This is done by playing the scale up, down, up, down, etc. , non-stop, for several minutes at a time. You will notice finger muscles, hand muscles and arm muscles you never knew you had.

When you are capable of playing the scale at 208, two notes per "click", non-stop for five (5) minutes, you have crossed the finish line of the marathon scale. The speed you developed on this one scale is quickly and easily transferred to any of the other scales. Plan on taking as long as one year to finish the marathon scale. Plan on enjoying the benefits derived from the marathon scale for the rest of your piano-playing life.

SIGHT-READING

"As written" sight-reading is another area you should begin working. As the name implies, sight-reading is simply reading music on sight. There are many advantages derived from practicing sight-reading. Sight-reading will:

1.) increase the speed at which you are able to read notes
2.) improve fingering ability
3.) assist you in noticing and using melodic, harmonic and rhythmic patterns
4,) make all of your "as written" and "chord symbol" practice more efficient
5.) develop confidence

A hymnal presents ideal material on which to begin your sight-reading practice.

Before you actually begin sight-reading a piece of music, take sixty seconds to look it over. Do not play anything during this minute. Notice the title, composer, style marking, key signature, time signature and rhythm level. Look for repeats, unusual rhythms, unusual chords, difficult melodic passages, difficult finger patterns, improbabilities and impossibilities.

The title of the music should be noticed because you might recognize the song, hence, your ear may be used to advantage.

The composer should be noticed because stylistic differences exist among composers.

The style marking indicates the speed and/or mood of the music. When written, it is found in the upper left corner of the first page. (Hymns usually contain no style marking.) While you should be aware of the style marking, don't be afraid to modify it, when necessary. For example, you may choose to slow the speed of a fast song, thus allowing you to maintain a steady beat.

The top number of the time signature tells you how many beats are in each measure. The bottom number tells you which type of note gets one beat.

The rhythm level tells you whether you are dealing with whole beats, half beats or quarter beats.

You should locate repeats so that you will know where to go back, to begin any repeats. A repeat may occur in the form of a repeat sign, a D.S. (Dal Segno) or a D.C. (Da Capo).

You should locate unusual rhythms, unusual chords, difficult melodic passages and difficult finger patterns so that you may work your way through them mentally, before the "real McCoy". This may involve "touch-practice" (i.e. touching the piano keys without actually pressing them down).

Improbabilities are anything wickedly different, such as both hands suddenly reading in treble clef, both hands suddenly reading in bass clef, a time signature of $\frac{6}{4}$, etc.

Impossibilities include anything you know you can't handle, such as tenths in the bass, when you know your left hand is only capable of spanning nine notes.

Modify impossibilities so that you are able to play the music. The rules for modification are simple: if you choose not to "roll" an interval or chord (i.e. play the notes, from lowest to highest, in extremely rapid, even succession), play only the lowest note (or notes) you are able to reach with your left hand; play only the highest note (or notes) you are able to reach with your right hand,

I recommend that you practice sight-reading hands separately for several weeks (or months?) before you begin sight-reading hands together.

Remember: all music contains patterns. A pattern is any of the following:

- exact repeats and modified repeats of small segments of music
- notes and/or rhythms which function in a sequence
- a group of notes and/or rhythms which have similar characteristics
- a group of notes and/or rhythms which function as a unit

Noticing melodic, harmonic and rhythmic patterns will make sight-reading much easier.

Avoid "false starts" (i.e. starting, stopping, going back, starting, stopping, going back, etc.), Avoid "hesitations" (i.e. pauses, between beats or portions of beats). Correct rhythm is infinitely more important than correct notes. Maintain a steady beat at all cost.

MEMORIZATION

Memorization is learning to play music, originally learned from a written page, without a written page. Because memorization frees you from the written page, it is a great way to add spontaneity to your "as written" and "chord symbol" performance.

Sometimes, memorization happens quite naturally. You sit down to practice a song and suddenly realize that you are ignoring the written page of music. However, when you want to memorize a particular song, and the memorization does not happen naturally, I recommend using some memorization techniques.

First, let's understand how the memorization process works.

Memorization takes place three ways:

1.) through muscle memory
2.) through aural memory
3.) through pattern memory

MUSCLE MEMORY

All muscles contain memory. Your finger muscles develop memory through repetition. While repetition is considered, by many, to be a dull way to practice, the resultant finger memory creates a pianist's delight: the pleasure of watching your fingers perform music, with little or no conscious mental control.

AURAL MEMORY

Your ears are excellent memorization devices. They develop memory from listening. (...what ears do best) Acute listening abilities are developed through ear training exercises and/or actually playing by ear. While repetition is an aural memory aid, it won't replace acute listening. The more perceptive your listening capabilities become, the more you will be able to use your ears as memorization devices.

PATTERN MEMORY

All music contains patterns. Noticing melodic, harmonic and rhythmic patterns will make memorization much easier. You simply "hop on" when the pattern begins and "hop off" when the pattern ends, thus allowing you to quickly and easily remember several measures of music. When using pattern memory, you will probably visualize the written page in your mind, though keyboard visualization may come into play.

You may use muscle memory, aural memory and pattern memory simultaneously. Each supports the others. When memorizing for a public performance, you should be so thorough that you're able to visualize the written page in your mind. Using only muscle memory for a public performance is very dangerous because stage fright may cause some muscle memory lapse. While aural memory is safer in a performance situation, it should not be relied on alone, for the same reason. The best way to memorize music is to make a conscious effort to incorporate all three: muscle memory, aural memory and pattern memory.

Memorization techniques enhance muscle memory, aural memory and pattern memory. The most commonly used memorization technique is repetition. Another is section-work. This entails beginning the song from memory, playing until you get stuck, then practicing the section of music where you got stuck (using the written page). This procedure is repeated until you are able to play through the music entirely from memory. Yet another memorization technique is intermittent practice. This is especially useful when you must memorize something quickly. Practice section-work for five to fifteen minutes, then leave the piano completely. Do something else for thirty minutes or more. Return to your section-work for five to fifteen minutes, then leave the piano completely. Do something else for thirty minutes or more. Keep repeating this procedure. During the thirty minutes or more that your mind is occupied with something else, your subconscious is ingesting the material covered in the five to fifteen minute practice session. Intermittent practice teams your conscious with your subconscious to speed up results.

NOW...ABOUT TECHNIQUE

"Technique" (also spelled "technic") is a general term used to describe the physical (or mechanical) skills involved in performance. The three interrelated aspects of technique are: endurance, speed and control. Basically, building endurance develops speed which, in turn, brings about or expands control. However, there is a lot more to technique than the previous oversimplified statement suggests. Let's look at each aspect more closely.

Endurance is perseverance — enduring the hardship of physical pain and mental agony that is sometime required to develop the ability to: 1.) play virtually non-stop for long periods of time; 2.) handle tempo (i.e. rate of speed) extremes; 3.) handle (either separately or in combination between the hands) the various aspects of shading: style, phrasing, fast, slow, loud and soft. As such, endurance can be thought of as a launching pad for the development of technique.

When the word "speed" is used, we tend to think "fast". While developing the ability to play notes in rapid, even succession is both a product of endurance and an integral part of technique, so is developing the ability to play notes in an extremely slow and even succession. Speed can be thought of as our fueled rocket.

Control is the sought-after end result of technical study. Fingers capable of doing whatever the ear hears, or the mind demands, are exercising control over a piano keyboard. To complete our analogy, control can be thought of as the instrument panel used to guide our rocket through whatever environments we encounter.

Every musician worth at least his weight in salt is keenly aware of his own technical limitations and is constantly seeking to break down technical barriers through the fine art known to us all as....practice.

SOME PRACTICAL TECHNICAL EXERCISES

This first little nifty notation, called a "balance exercise", develops independence between the hands. At first, the right hand plays double forte while the left hand plays double piano. Then, in the third measure, the hands abruptly switch volume.

To learn this balance exercise, you will find it helpful to practice some preparatory steps, 1.) Practice the first two measures as a section. Have your right hand play normal volume while your left hand touches (but does not press down) each of its notes. Gradually increase the volume of the right hand notes, still maintaining just the touch on each individual left hand note. Go slowly. When your right hand is a good strong double forte, begin pressing down the left hand notes, just enough to get them to sound. Congratulations! Your right hand is now able to play loudly while your left hand plays softly. 2.) Practice the third and fourth measures as a section, following the same process. When your left hand is capable of playing loudly while your right hand plays softly, you are ready to tackle the entire exercise. Remember to go slowly!

Here's a variation on the balance exercise:

If, at first, you find this variation quite impossible, use whole notes in place of the quarter notes. Gradually add speed until you arrive at a tempo which approximates quarter notes.

Both the balance exercise and its variation are extremely useful. You will find a lot of music, especially of the classical variety, which calls for differences in volume and/or phrasing between the hands.

If you're a true glutton for punishment, go for this one:

EMBELLISHMENTS

Musicians use embellishments (also called "ornaments") to adorn a melody or a harmony. An embellishment may be a single note or a group of notes.

(Note: Use the nails of the third and fourth fingers when going up in the right hand. Use the thumb nail when coming down. Hold the fingers quite firmly at about a forty-five degree angle; lead ahead with the wrist and let the fingers drag behind.)

A <u>roll</u> is written:  and played:

A <u>trill</u> is written:  or: or:

and played:

A <u>tremelo</u> is written:  and played:

or written:  and played:

A <u>mor</u>dent is written:  and played:

* An "<u>inverted</u> <u>mor</u>dent" is written:  and played:

A <u>double</u> <u>mordent</u> is written:  and played:

* The term "inverted mordent" was never used during the Baroque period. The symbol ∿ indicates a <u>trill</u> which begins on the auxiliary note.

A <u>turn</u> is written:

and played:

In closing, I'll share one final observation: The ornaments and the symbols used to indicate ornaments vary somewhat depending on which period (time-frame) a piece of music was written. Also, with each new discovery of an old manuscript, new interpretations evolve.

Scholarly research continues...

CHAPTER SIX
INTERMEDIATE THEORY

LOWERED INTERVALS

The intervals we learned in chapter three are called "perfect intervals" (4th, 5th and 8th) and "major intervals" (2nd, 3rd, 6th and 7th). Now let's include "diminished intervals" and "minor intervals".

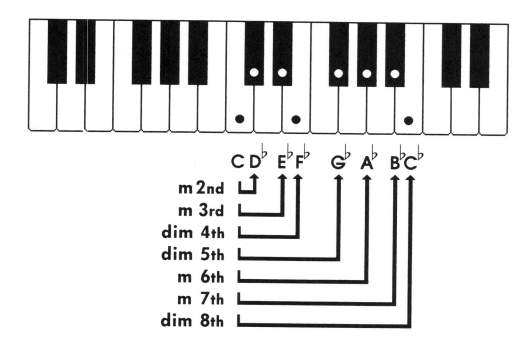

As you can see, diminished intervals are formed by lowering the top note of any perfect interval one half step, and minor intervals are formed by lowering the top note of any major interval one half step. Because the diminished 4th yields the sound of a major 3rd, and the diminished 8th yields the sound of a major 7th, you really have only five new sounds with which to acquaint yourself. [Note: The appendix (page 216) completely explains the classification of intervals — and may I recommend combining it with some cookies and milk to ward off "the dulls".]

CHORDS

The bad news: There are thousands of chords to be learned on the piano.

Better news: There are approximately forty commonly used chords.

The good news: The seven chord "recipes" found on the next page will allow you to play 98% of the chords you will find in music. The remaining 2% (approximately one chord in fifty) are called "special instruction" chords. We'll cover these too.

First, here are the seven chord recipes:

Triads
{
Major – skip 3, then skip 2

Minor – skip 2, then skip 3

Diminished – skip 2, then skip 2

Augmented – skip 3, then skip 3
}

Sevenths
{
Seventh – major chord and the note that is one whole step down from the octave

Major Seventh – major chord and the note that is one half step down from the octave

Minor Seventh – minor chord and the note that is one whole step down from the octave
}

The triads are explained in chapter three. If you don't understand them, have some fun reviewing chapter three. The seventh chords are new arrivals. Here's how they work:

The <u>seventh</u> chord (also known as "dominant seventh chord") contains four notes. The first three notes form a major chord. So, when you are forming a seventh chord on the note C, your first three notes will be C, E and G. To find the fourth note of this chord, go up (to the right) one octave from the bottom note (in this case, the bottom note is C, so you will go up to the next C), and come down (to the left) one whole step. This will put you on the note Bb.

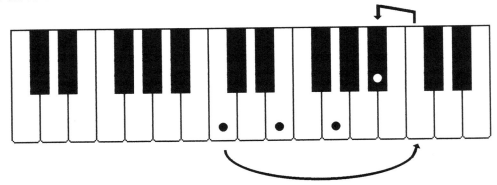

Play all four notes simultaneously and you will hear the sound of a C seventh chord. Be sure to use only the first, second, third and fifth fingers of either hand when playing this or any other seventh chord.

Using these fingers makes each chord member more accessible, hence, the full chord is more easily played.

The <u>major</u> <u>seventh</u> chord contains four notes. The first three notes form a major chord. So, when you are forming a major seventh chord on the note C, your first three notes will be C, E and G. To find the fourth note of this chord, go up one octave from the bottom note and come down one half step. This will put you on the note B.

Play all four notes simultaneously and you will hear the sound of a C major seventh chord.

The <u>minor</u> <u>seventh</u> chord contains four notes. The first three notes form a minor chord. So, when you are forming a minor seventh chord on the note C, your first notes will be C, Eb and G. To find the fourth note of this chord, go up one octave from the bottom note and come down one whole step. This will put you on the note Bb.

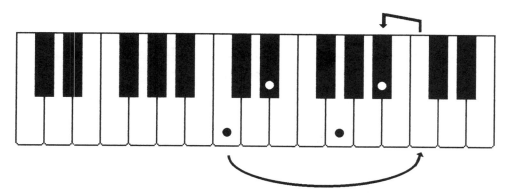

Play all four notes simultaneously and you will hear the sound of a C minor seventh chord.

Choose different notes on which to form these three types of seventh chords. Remember to use only the first, second, third and fifth fingers of either hand.

We can now abbreviate the seven chord recipes this way:

Using C as an example, the
chord symbols are written:

Major – 3, 2   C
Minor – 2, 3   Cm
Diminished – 2, 2   Cdim or C°
Augmented – 3, 3   Caug or C+ or C(#5)
Seventh – 3, 2 whole step   C7
Major Seventh – 3, 2 half step   Cmaj7
Minor Seventh – 2, 3 whole step   Cm7

The seventh chord is also known as a "dominant seventh" because it has very strong tendencies. It is a "chord of action". As such, it almost always demands to be resolved (i.e. move on to another chord). It contains the major triad and the minor seventh interval, and, as such, is really part major and part minor. The rule in music is: "the seventh is assumed to be minor", referring to this interval of the minor seventh. The chord symbol used to denote the dominant seventh chord is a letter and the number 7. So, "C7" means to play a dominant seventh starting on the note C.

The major seventh chord does not have very strong tendencies. It is a "chord of repose". As such, it does not demand to be resolved. This chord is called a "major seventh" because it contains the major seventh interval. The chord symbol used to denote the major seventh chord is a letter, followed by "maj7". So, "Cmaj7" means to play a major seventh chord starting on the note C.

The minor seventh chord functions equally well as either a "chord of action" or a "chord of repose". This chord is called a "minor seventh" because it contains the minor triad, not because it contains the minor seventh interval. (Remember: the seventh is assumed to be minor.) The chord symbol used to denote the minor seventh chord is a letter, followed by "m7". So, "Cm7" means to play a minor seventh chord starting on the note C.

In summary, C7 contains a minor seventh interval because the seventh is assumed to be minor. The "maj" in Cmaj7 refers to the seventh being raised, thereby creating a major seventh interval. The "m" in Cm7 refers to the third being lowered, thereby creating a minor triad.

SPECIAL INSTRUCTION CHORDS

Now that you are capable of forming 98% of the chords you will encounter, let's cover the special instruction chords. Rather than becoming proficient at these 2%ers, I recommend just reading through, forming them once or twice, and letting it go at that. While there are many different types of special instruction chords, they occur so rarely in music, that you can just look up the few you happen to bump into. From playing them (and getting tired of looking them up), you will gradually begin to remember these colorful chords. In this chapter, I will cover only the most common special instruction chords. You will find a complete list in chapter eight.

There are ten common special instruction chords. Using C as an example, they look like this:

Csus	also written as: Csus4
C6	
Cm6	
C7sus	also written as: C7sus4
C7(#5)	also written as: C7(+5) or C7+
C7(b5)	also written as: C7(-5)
Cm7(b5)	also written as: CØ7
C°7	also written as: Cdim7
Cm(#7)	also written as: Cm(+7)
C/D	also written as: C/D bass or $\frac{C}{D}$

There is one common special instruction which isn't a chord:

N.C.	also written as: No Chord

Remember: chord members get their names from their relationship to the scale. The "root" of a chord is the same as the first note of the scale. For example: the root of a C chord is the note C, which is the first note of the C scale. The "third" of a chord is the same note as the third note of the scale. For example: the third of a C chord is the note E, which is the third note of the C scale. The "fifth" of a chord is the same note as the fifth note of the scale. For example: the fifth of a C chord is the note G, which is the fifth note of the C scale.

The numbers contained in chord symbols refer to chord members. Because chord members get their names from their relationship to the scale, you can be sure that when you see the number 4 in a chord symbol, the fourth note of the scale is included in that chord. You can be sure that when you see the number 6 in a chord symbol, the sixth note of the scale is included in that chord. The single exception to this rule is the number 7 because, as you remember, the seventh is assumed to be a minor interval. For example: the seventh note of the C scale is the note B, but a C7 chord contains the notes C, E, G and Bb. C to Bb is the "assumed" minor seventh interval.

Let's start with the Csus chord. The "sus" refers to the word "suspended", meaning that the chord has a "hanging" sound. It wants to resolve (i.e. move on to another chord). This suspended sound is created by replacing the third of the chord with the fourth. So a sus chord contains only the root, fourth and fifth. For example: a Csus chord is made up of the notes C, F and G. Just remember "sus" means "fourth replaces third".

The C6 chord is simply a C major chord with the sixth note of the scale stacked on top. So a C6 chord contains C (the root), E (the third), G (the fifth) and A (the sixth). Dadgum! That's simple!

The Cm6 (pronounced "C minor sixth") is simply a C minor chord with the sixth note of the scale stacked on top. So a Cm6 chord contains the notes C, Eb, G and A.

The C7sus is a C7 chord with a suspended fourth. So a C7sus contains the notes C, F, G and Bb.

The C7(#5) is a C7 chord with one difference: the fifth is sharped. So G is replaced by G#. The notes in this chord are C, E, G# and Bb.

The C7(b5) is a C7 chord with one difference: the fifth is flatted. So G is replaced by Gb. The notes in this chord are C, E, Gb and Bb.

The Cm7(b5) is a Cm7 chord with one difference: the fifth is flatted. So G is replaced by Gb. The notes in this chord are C, Eb, Gb and Bb. This chord is also known as a Cø7 (C half diminished seventh) because C, Eb and Gb form a diminished triad and C to Bb form a minor seventh interval. Because part of this chord is diminished (the triad) and part of this chord is minor (the minor seventh interval), musicians have come to call this a "half diminished seventh" chord. (Yes, they could have called it a "half minor seventh" chord. But they didn't. So don't ask crazy questions.)

The C°7 (C full diminished seventh) is a diminished triad and a diminished seventh interval. The notes in this chord are C, Eb, Gb and Bbb (B double flat). C to B is a major seventh interval; C to Bb is a minor seventh interval; C to Bbb is a diminished seventh interval. Since Bbb is the same note as A, quite often you will see this chord mis-spelled as C, Eb, Gb and A. Either way, the correct notes sound and the chord is successfully played.

The Cm(#7) is a Cm chord with a raised seventh stacked on top. A Cm7 chord is made up of the notes C, Eb, G and Bb. When we sharp the seventh for the Cm(#7) chord, we simply raise the Bb to B. So the notes in this chord are C, Eb, G and B. Play the Cm(#7) softly and it sounds like a soap opera is about to break for an advertisement.

The C/D chord is called a "false root". The letter C in this chord symbol tells you to play a C major chord. The "/D" tells you to play the note D as the bass note (bottom-most note) in your left hand. So "C" refers to a chord and "/D" refers to a single note. The root (bottom note) of a C chord is the note C. When we replace this bottom note with any other note, we are replacing the real root of this chord with a "false root". The C/D chord is pronounced: "C with a D in the bass", The notes in this chord are D, C, E and G.

False root chords are very colorful. In fact, the chord actually heard by the listener is much more complex than what the performer reads. This is because the listener hears the false root as the real root of the chord. Using C/D as an example, the listener hears a D11 (no 5, no 3) chord. All the performer reads is "C/D". Now, I'd say that's quite nifty! What a good deal for the performer! What a good deal for the listener! (I guess you can tell that I like false root chords.)

The last special instruction I will cover in this chapter is not a chord. "N.C." stands for "No Chord". N.C. tells you to release any chord you may be holding down. N.C. also tells you to not play anything even remotely resembling harmony until the next chord symbol. I hope the fine folks who live in the state just north of South Carolina don't mind sharing this abbreviation with us. To musicians, N.C. is like a short drink of water during a long chordal hike.

MUSIC SYSTEMS

I have learned a lot of useless theory in my time. For example, understanding the difference between the German 6/5 augmented sixth chord and the French 4/3 augmented sixth chord has not had a profound effect on the direction of my musical career.

Know this: I will not relate any impractical theory knowledge to you. I will give you only the music theory which I have found useful in my performance. After all, music listeners, generally, are not interested in your theory knowledge. They are interested in hearing the performance resulting from your knowledge of music theory. So, any music theory which is not made to relate to performance, in my opinion, becomes useless knowledge.

There are five music systems. I will explain them, and then demonstrate the ways each system is practically applied in performance.

The music systems are:

  1.) Circle Of Fifths
  2.) Figured Bass
  3.) Chord Scales
  4.) Non-Harmonic Tones
  5.) Modes

I will cover the first two at the intermediate level, and the last three at the advanced level.

CIRCLE OF FIFTHS

Key signatures tell you which notes are sharped or flatted in the music you play. As such, they help orient you to the notes being used in the music you play. The more familiar you are with key signatures, the more likely you are to strike the right notes. If avoiding wrong notes sounds like a really good idea, then dadburnit, know your key signatures — learn about the circle of fifths!

99.9% of all music is tonal (i.e. centered around one tone). This means, probably 100% of all the music you will ever perform, whether by note, by chord symbol or by ear, will be tonal music. The key signature of a song tells you which tone (i.e. note) that song is centered around. If knowing this "home base" note sounds like a really good idea, then dadgummit, know your key signatures — learn about the circle of fifths!

Circle of fifths is an explanation of the 12 major key signatures and the 12 minor key signatures, demonstrating each key signature's relationship to all the other key signatures.

We simply start with the first note of the most accessible major scale on the piano keyboard: C. Then we go up a fifth. This puts us on the note G. We go up a fifth from G. This puts us on the note D. We go up a fifth from D....and so on, until we circle back to C. Here's what it looks like:

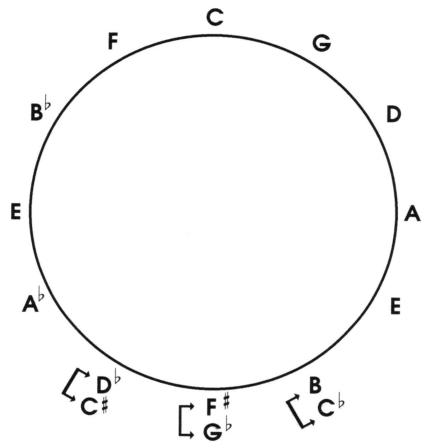

This gives us the 12 different notes found on the piano keyboard, locked into a pattern of successive fifths. The significance is this: the key of C contains no sharps or flats. The key of G contains 1 sharp. The key of D contains 2 sharps. The key of A contains 3 sharps; the key of E, 4 sharps; the key of B, 5 sharps; the key of F#, 6 sharps. The note F# is also known as Gb. The key of Gb contains 6 flats; the key of Db, 5 flats; the key of Ab, 4 flats; the key of Eb, 3 flats; the key of Bb, 2 flats; the key of F, 1 flat; and a partridge in a pear tree.

Now the pattern looks like this:

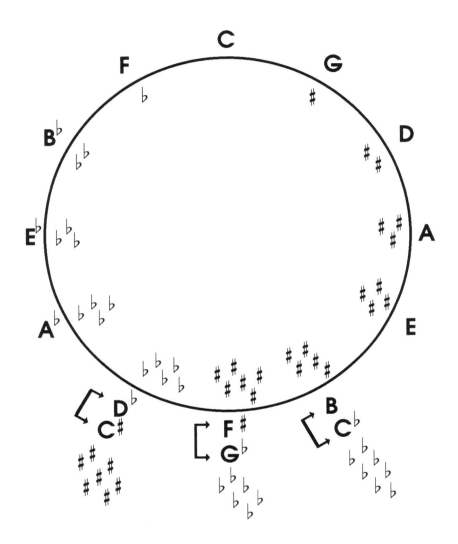

Since there are 12 different notes on the piano keyboard, there are 12 different major keys on the piano keyboard: one for each note. This, of course, also means there are 12 different minor keys on the piano keyboard: one for each note.

Because the A minor scale has the same key signature as C major (no sharps or flats), the minor circle of fifths starts with the key of A minor:

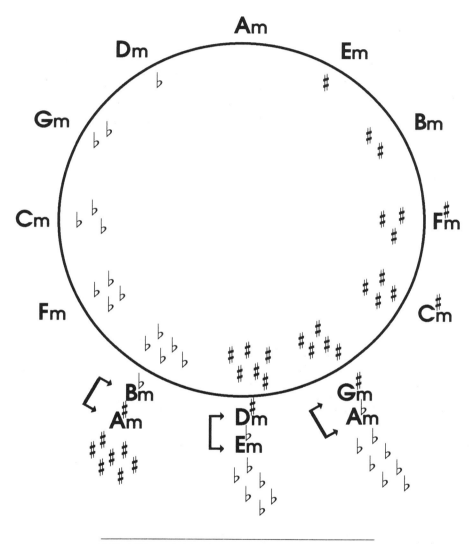

RELATIVE MINOR – RELATIVE MAJOR

With 12 major keys and 12 minor keys, we have a total of 24 different keys. Yet, we have only 12 different key signatures because each minor key shares a key signature with a major key. Because the key of A minor shares the same key signature with the key of C major, we say A minor is the "relative minor" to C major. This, of course, means C major is the relative major to A minor. (What a revelation!)

Likewise, E minor is the relative minor to G major and G major is the relative major to E minor. B minor is the relative minor to D major and D major is the relative major to B minor....and so on, through the entire circle of fifths.

You may use the piano keyboard to find the relative minor of any major key. Simply skip two notes (a minor 3rd) down:

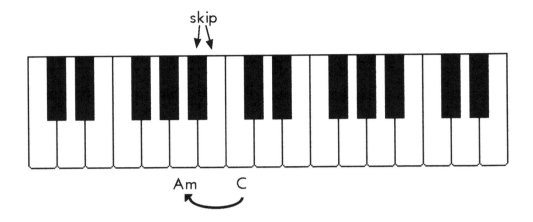

Conversely, you may use the piano keyboard to find the relative major of any minor key. Simply skip two notes (a minor 3rd) up:

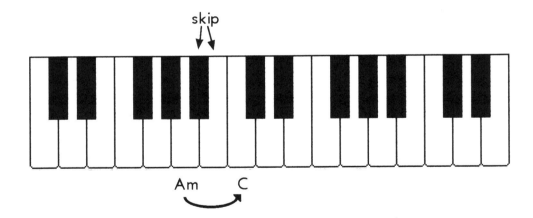

The obvious question: How do you know whether you are in the major key or its relative minor? The last chord of any song usually reveals the answer: When the last chord is major, you are probably in the major key; when the last chord is minor, you are probably in the minor key. (An item known as a "Picardy third" is the main exception to this rule. It will be explained when we get to figured bass.)

A SHORT CUT

Memorizing the circle of fifths is dull work. So don't bother. Instead, when you wish to ascertain what key your music is in, use a dandy and handy short cut.

When you are dealing with a key signature which contains sharps, simply go up to the next note from the last sharp in the key signature. For example, the key signature with 1 sharp:

The last sharp in this key signature is F#. (Yes, it's also the first sharp and the only sharp.) Go to the next note up from F#. You are in the key of G major (or G major's relative minor).

The key signature with 2 sharps:

The last sharp is C#. The next note up is D, so we are in the key of D major (or D major's relative minor).

The key signature with 6 sharps is tricky:

The last sharp is E#. (E# is the same note as F.) The next note up from E# is F#. So 6 sharps is the key of F# major (or F# major's relative minor).

When you are dealing with a key signature which contains flats, the flat before the last flat (the penultimate flat) is the key. For example, the key signature with 6 flats:

Gb is the penultimate flat, so we are in the key of Gb major (or Gb major's relative minor).

The key signature with 2 flats:

Bb is the penultimate flat, so we are in the key of Bb major (or Bb major's relative minor).

Since the key signature with 1 flat has no penultimate flat, you just have to remember: 1 flat is the key of F major (or F major's relative minor). You can handle this.

PRACTICAL APPLICATION OF THE CIRCLE OF FIFTHS

Knowing the circle of fifths gives you insight into key signatures. Contemplating the key signature of a song, before you play it, gives you a big advantage: You know (with the exception of accidentals) which notes are going to be used in the song. Say, for example, you are in the key of Eb major. You go head-hunting for the notes Eb, F, G, Ab, Bb, C and D. To any note, other than these seven, you might cast a suspicious glance, before you play it. You know any note, other than these seven, represents a temporary departure from the key of Eb and, as such, deserves scrutiny.

The importance of the circle of fifths, as it applies to tonal music, will become evident as you study and begin to use the next music system: figured bass. For now, practice using the circle of fifths by going through a music book or two, pencil in hand, labeling the key signatures of each song and key changes, if any, within each song.

For all those people who might say, "There is one circle of fifths for major keys and another circle of fifths for minor keys, so this music system should be called the circles of fifths", I have two things to say to you: 1.) Your right. 2.) Quit being so picky.

FIGURED BASS

The name "Figured Bass" refers to figures written above or below the bass clef. These figures are Roman numerals, and they refer to chords built on the notes of a scale. Say, for example, you are in the key of C. The Roman numeral one (I) would refer to the chord built on the first note of the C scale: the C chord. The Roman numeral four (IV) would refer to the chord built on the fourth note of the C scale: the F chord.

Musicians use upper case Roman numerals to refer to major chords, lower case Roman numerals to refer to minor chords, lower case Roman numerals with a little zero (on the right) to refer to diminished chords and upper case Roman numerals with a little plus sign (on the right) to refer to augmented chords. Since there are seven different notes in each scale, only Roman numerals one (I) through seven (VII) are necessary.
Major chords are denoted using these symbols:

$$I \quad II \quad III \quad IV \quad V \quad VI \quad VII$$

Minor chords are denoted using these symbols:

$$i \quad ii \quad iii \quad iv \quad v \quad vi \quad vii$$

Diminished chords are denoted using these symbols:

$$i^{\circ} \quad ii^{\circ} \quad iii^{\circ} \quad iv^{\circ} \quad v^{\circ} \quad vi^{\circ} \quad vii^{\circ}$$

Augmented chords are denoted using these symbols:

$$I^{+} \quad II^{+} \quad III^{+} \quad IV^{+} \quad V^{+} \quad VI^{+} \quad VII^{+}$$

Because all major scales are formed from the same pattern (W W H W W W H), there are figured bass symbols which are standard for all major keys. We call these symbols "standard figured bass". The standard figured bass for all major keys is:

$$I \quad ii \quad iii \quad IV \quad V \quad vi \quad vii^{\circ}$$

Using the key of C as an example:

Figured Bass Symbol:	I	ii	iii	IV	V	vi	vii$^{\circ}$
Chord Symbol:	C	Dm	Em	F	G	Am	Bdim

Using the key of G as an example:

Figured Bass Symbol:	I	ii	iii	IV	V	vi	vii°
Chord Symbol:	G	Am	Bm	C	D	Em	F#dim

I was surprised to learn that there are more non-major chords in major keys than there are major chords, and that there are as many minor chords in major keys as there are major chords in major keys. However, my surprise was diminished (no pun intended) when I realized that the major chords occupy the key (pun intended) I, IV and V positions. Since I, IV and V are the only major chords in any major key, and because I, IV and V are the strongest (i.e. most important) chords in all major keys, we musicians have given them a special designation: "principal chords".

Because all natural minor scales are formed from the same pattern (W H W W H W W), there are figured bass symbols which are standard for all natural minor keys. Again, we call these symbols "standard figured bass". The standard figured bass for all natural minor keys is:

	i	ii°	III	iv	v	VI	VII

Using the key of A minor as an example:

Figured Bass Symbol:	i	ii°	III	iv	v	VI	VII
Chord Symbol:	Am	Bdim	C	Dm	Em	F	G

Using the key of E minor as an example:

Figured Bass Symbol:	i	ii°	III	iv	v	VI	VII
Chord Symbol:	Em	F#dim	G	Am	Bm	C	D

Notice that the minor chords (i, iv and v) occupy the most important positions.

SCALE DEGREES

Now let's look at the names given to scale degrees (i.e. notes in a scale). The first scale degree (i.e. the first note of a scale) is called "tonic". It is the most important note of a scale because it is the central note around which melody is written. The triad which is built on this scale degree is called the "tonic triad". It is the central chord around which harmony is constructed. Music returns to tonic for a sense of rest and finality.

You could say that what tonic is to a musician, is a lot like what home base is to a baseball player: a great place to start and the place you usually hope to end up.

The fifth scale degree is called "dominant" because of the powerful role it plays in melody and harmony. It is the second most important note of a scale. The triad which is built on this scale degree is the "dominant triad". It is the second most important chord.

The fourth scale degree is called "subdominant", not because its position is just below the dominant, but because it is located a fifth <u>below</u> tonic (i.e. the "under dominant"), as opposed to dominant, which is located a fifth <u>above</u> tonic. Subdominant is the third most important note of the scale. The triad which is built on this scale degree is called the "subdominant triad". It is the third most important chord.

The second scale degree is called "supertonic" because it is located on the note just above tonic. The third scale degree is called "mediant" because it is halfway between tonic and dominant. The sixth scale degree is called "submediant" because it is halfway between subdominant and tonic (IV V vi vii° I). The seventh scale degree is called "leading tone" because it has a tendency to lead to tonic.

I	tonic
ii	supertonic
iii	mediant
IV	subdominant
V	dominant
vi	submediant
vii°	leading tone

ii, iii, vi and vii° function like weak versions of either I, IV or V. Here's how:

When different chords contain some of the same notes, we say these chords contain "common tones" (i.e. notes common to both chords). Two different chords may contain any number of common tones. For example, the C and G chords contain one common tone: the note G. The F and Dm chords contain two common tones: the notes F and A. The C and Dm chords contain no common tones. The C6 and Am7 chords contain all common tones: the notes C, E, G and A.

The more notes two chords have in common, the more similar they become, and the more likely they are to be used interchangeably. The iii chord shares two common tones with the I chord, hence, it is sometimes used in place of the I chord, as a weaker version of the I chord. In other words, the iii chord is capable of functioning as a weak tonic triad.

iii and vi are said to be "replacement chords" for the I chord. What this means is: when a composer gets tired of seeing the same old I chord in his music, he will just slip in a vi or a iii chord as a replacement. He may also consider using the iii or vi chord when he wants a "watered down" I chord.

For all the same reasons, ii and vi are replacement chords for the IV chord — that is, ii and vi are each capable of functioning as weaker versions of the subdominant triad. And, for all the same reasons, vii° and iii are replacement chords for the V chord — that is, vii° and iii are each capable of functioning as weaker versions of the dominant triad. Isn't this exciting stuff? (Don't answer that.)

So, ii, iii, vi and vii° impersonate either I, IV or V.

PRINCIPAL CHORD	REPLACEMENT CHORDS	
I	vi	iii
IV	ii	vi
V	iii	vii°

Notice the vi chord is capable of impersonating either I or IV and the iii chord is capable of impersonating either I or V. The ii chord functions only as a weak subdominant and the vii° chord functions only as a weak dominant.

PRACTICAL APPLICATION OF FIGURED BASS

Understanding figured bass allows us to analyze harmony. Having the ability to analyze harmony makes learning music much easier because harmonic patterns (such as I vi IV V I or I IV V IV I) become obvious. Having the ability to analyze harmony also makes creating music much easier. This is because harmonic analysis develops an understanding of how chords are put together to form a harmony.

A thorough understanding of figured bass will have a profound effect on your ability to : 1.) practice
2.) memorize
3.) sight-read
4.) play by ear
5.) compose
6.) arrange
7.) improvise (compose music at the same time you are performing it)
8.) transpose (change an entire song from one key to another)
9.) modulate (move from one key to another within a song)

Begin using figured bass by analyzing the harmony of some favorite "chord symbol" songs. Here's the easiest way to do this:

Find out what key you are in by using the circle of fifths charts or by using the short cut I mentioned. You will find one major key with your song's key signature and one minor key with your song's key signature. If the very last chord of your song is major, you you are probably in the major key. Likewise, if the very last chord of your song is minor, you are probably in the minor key. (The main exception to this rule is a "Picardy third", where the major tonic triad appears at the end of a song that is otherwise in a minor key.) To be absolutely certain of which key you are dealing with, look for the song's first-occurring tonic chord. If the major key's tonic chord occurs before the minor key's tonic chord (the minor key's tonic chord might not occur at all), you are in the major key. Conversely, if the minor key's tonic chord occurs before the major key's tonic chord (the major key's tonic chord might not occur at all), you are in the minor key. Be sure the song you have chosen remains in the same key throughout.

If your song is written in major, write the standard figured bass for major keys (I ii iii IV V vi vii°) at the top of the first page. If your song is written in minor, write the standard figured bass for minor keys (i ii° III iv v VI VII) at the top of the first page. Now fill in the corresponding chord symbols for each figured bass symbol. For example, if your song is in the key of D major, you will write this:

I	ii	iii	IV	V	vi	vii°
D	Em	F#m	G	A	Bm	C#dim

If your song is in the key of D minor, you will write this:

i	ii°	III	iv	v	VI	VII
Dm	Edim	F	Gm	Am	Bb	C

Now simply go through the song, with pencil in hand, writing the corresponding figured bass symbol above each chord symbol. Circle any chord which does not comply with standard figured bass. I will show you how to analyze these non-complying chords later.

To analyze false root chords, you must first determine whether or not the false root, itself, is a member of the triad. If it is a member of the triad, you are dealing with an inversion. For example: C/E is used to indicate a 1st inversion C chord. C/G is used to indicate a 2nd inversion C chord. When doing figured bass analysis, both C/E and C/G should be analyzed as C chords, because the ear hears them as inverted C chords. If the false root, itself, is not a member of the triad, it is the real root of the chord. For example: C/F. Since the note F is not a member of the C triad, the note F is the root of this chord. C/F is used to indicate a Fmaj9 (no 3rd) chord. When doing figured bass analysis, C/F should be analyzed as an F chord, because the ear hears it as a F chord.

When you have gone through the whole song, go back and see if you are able to locate any harmonic patterns. After you have analyzed several songs this way, see if you are able to locate any harmonic patterns which are similar, from one song to another. You will definitely notice one thing: an abundance of tonic, subdominant and dominant chords.

When you want to analyze songs which contain changes in key, simply re-write the standard figured bass, with the corresponding chord symbols, at the key change.

If you would like to analyze songs which do not contain chord symbols (i.e. "as written" songs), you must go through the notes of each beat, or groups of beats, to ascertain which chords are being used.

MUTATIONS

Any chord which does not comply with standard figured bass is a mutation. A mutation represents a temporary departure from the key (or mode) in which a song is written.

An example of a mutation is the use of a iv chord in a major key:

Another example of a mutation is the use of a I+ chord:

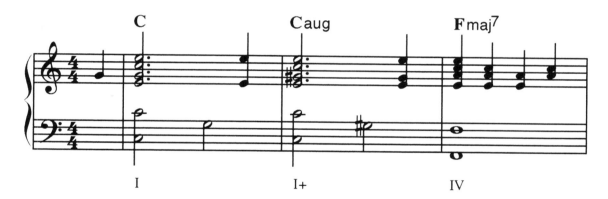

A composer's use of mutations is nothing more than poetic license. He decides that he wants to get from one part of the music to another, in a less-than-conventional way (i.e. by inserting chords which violate the key signature, hence they also violate the standard figured bass). This is not to say that mutations are uncommon (they aren't) or inherently bad (they aren't). Mutations occur many times in very lovely and sophisticated music.

MUTATIONS AND THE THREE FORMS OF MINOR

There is only one form of major. Major is major and that's that. However, there are three forms of minor: natural, harmonic and melodic.

Natural minor is the form of minor which is derived from the relative major.

As an example, here is the A natural minor scale:

And here are the resulting chord symbols and standard figured bass:

Am	Bdim	C	Dm	Em	F	G
i	ii°	III	iv	v	VI	VII

Natural minor is used much less often than the two forms of minor that are derived from it: harmonic and melodic.

Harmonic minor is identical to natural minor, except the seventh scale degree is sharped. This sharped seventh scale degree enhances the resultant harmonies, mostly because the dominant chord becomes major. Generally, we humans prefer the sound of a major dominant (which acts like a chord of action) over the sound of a minor dominant (which acts more like a chord of repose). We like our dominants to dominate!

Here is the A harmonic minor scale:

And here are the resulting chord symbols and figured bass:

Am	Bdim	Caug	Dm	E	F	G#dim
i	ii°	III+	iv	V	VI	#vii°

As a result of the sharped seventh scale degree, the III, v and VII chords (which occur in natural minor) are mutated (changed) to III+, V and #vii°.

Melodic minor has two versions: 1.) an ascending version which contains a sharped sixth scale degree and a sharped seventh scale degree and 2.) a descending version which is identical to natural minor. The use of the sixth interchangeably with the sharped seventh enhances the resultant melodies. It also gives the composer more harmonic choices.

Here is the A melodic minor scale:

And here are the resulting chord symbols and figured bass:

Am	Bdim or Bm	C or Caug	Dm or D	Em or E	F or F#dim	G or G#dim
i	ii° or ii	III or III+	iv or IV	v or V	VI or #vi°	VII or #vii°

As a result of allowing us to use either the sixth of the sharped sixth, and the seventh or the sharped seventh, melodic minor includes all the chord symbols and standard figured bass of natural minor plus these mutations: ii, III+, IV, V, #vi° and #vii°.

___

ALTERED SCALE DEGREE MUTATIONS

In music, the word "altered" means raised (sharped) or lowered (flatted). So, the term "altered scale degree" refers to any scale degree which has been raised or lowered. The #vii° chord found in harmonic minor and the #vi° and #vii° chords found in melodic minor are built on an altered scale degree. As such, we call them "altered scale degree chords". Here are the altered scale degree chords used in conjunction with major keys:

The flatted leading tone triad (bVII) contains a lowered root. For example: In the key of F, the note E from the Edim chord (vii°) is lowered to Eb, thereby creating an Eb major chord (bVII).

The flatted submediant triad (bVI) contains both a lowered root and a lowered fifth. For example: In the key of F, the notes D and A from the Dm chord (vi) are lowered to Db and Ab, thereby creating a Db major chord (bVI).

The flatted mediant triad (bIII) contains both a lowered root and a lowered fifth. For example: In the key of F, the notes A and E from the Am chord (iii) are lowered to Ab and Eb, thereby creating an Ab major chord (bIII).

The flatted supertonic triad (bII) also contains a lowered root and a lowered fifth. This chord is occasionally referred to as the "Neapolitan chord". Here is a notated example:

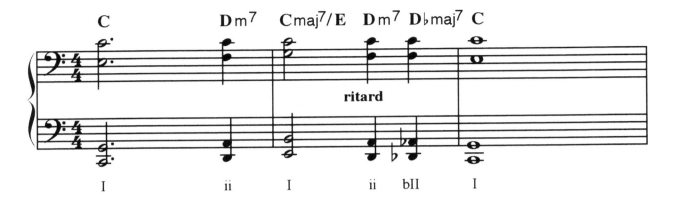

Because altered scale degree chords are a temporary departure from the key (or mode) and, as such, do not comply with standard figured bass, they are mutations.

SECONDARY DOMINANT MUTATIONS

Before we talk about secondary dominants, let's talk about the primary dominant. The primary dominant is dominant as we already know it: five scale degrees above tonic. So the term "primary dominant" is the specific way we musicians refer to the dominant of tonic ("V" or "V" of I" or "V/I")

Secondary dominants occur five scale degrees above any note other than tonic. Included under the term "secondary dominant" are:

– the dominant of supertonic (V of ii or V/ii) which is located five scale degrees above supertonic;
– the dominant of mediant (V of iii or V/iii) which is located five scale degrees above mediant;
– the dominant of subdominant (V of IV or V/IV) which is located five scale degrees above subdominant;
– the dominant of dominant (V of V or V/V) which is located five scale degrees above dominant;
– the dominant of submediant (V of vi or V/vi) which is located five scale degrees above submediant;
– the dominant of leading tone (V of vii.° or V/vii°) which is located five scale degrees above leading tone.

Secondary dominant chords are easily recognized because they are almost always dominant seventh chords. For example, in the key of C, G7 is the primary dominant seventh chord (V7 of I). Any dominant seventh chord which occurs, other than G7, is a secondary dominant. These include:

A7	(V7 of ii)
B7	(V7 of iii)
C7	(V7 of IV)
D7	(V7 of V)
E7	(V7 of vi)
F7	(V7 of either vii° or bVII)

However, secondary dominants are occasionally written as dominant triads. For example, in the key of C:

A	(V of ii)
B	(V of iii)
C	(tonic triad, but capable of functioning as V of IV)
D	(V of V)
E	(V of vi)
F	(subdominant triad, but capable of functioning as V of either vii° or bVII)

Secondary dominants, like all chords, are recognized by the company they keep. Look for the secondary dominant to resolve to a chord which is built on the note located five scale degrees below. For example, in the key of C:

Look for A7 to resolve to a chord built on D.
Look for B7 to resolve to a chord built on E.
Look for C7 to resolve to a chord built on F.
Look for D7 to resolve to a chord built on G.
Look for E7 to resolve to a chord built on A.
Look for F7 to resolve to a chord built on either B or Bb.

Occasionally, secondary dominants will resolve to a replacement chord of the chord which is built on the note located five scale degrees below. For example, in the key of C, D7 (V of V) might resolve to an Em chord (iii) instead of a G chord (V).

Secondary dominants may also resolve to another secondary dominant. For example, in the key of C: A7 (V7 of ii) resolving to D7 (V7 of V). In this situation, A7 is really functioning as the dominant of the dominant of the dominant (V7 of V7 of V).

Though we use the symbols "V of ii", "V of iii", etc. to analyze secondary dominants, what is really happening, when a secondary dominant occurs, is a short key change. We are temporarily in the key of the note located five scale degrees below the root of the secondary dominant. For example, in the key of C, D7 is analyzed as V7 of V. We call it a "secondary dominant" or "the dominant of the dominant". However, what our ear hears is a short key change to the key of G. (D7 is the primary dominant of the key of G.) What our ear hears is V7 of I in the key of G.

Because secondary dominants are a temporary departure from the key and, as such, do not comply with standard figured bass, they are mutations.

Whether primary or secondary, we humans like to hear dominants resolving. It has been said many times: "We live in a V7 to I world."

USING FIGURED BASS FOR TRANSPOSITION

This is simple! Say, for example, you are transposing a song from the key of G to the key of C, to accommodate the range of a vocalist you are accompanying. Start by doing a figured bass analysis of the song you wish to transpose. Then draw a cross-reference chart:

From:	G	Am	Bm	C	D	Em	F#dim
	I	ii	iii	IV	V	vi	vii°
To:	C	Dm	Em	F	G	Am	Bdim

Write the new chord symbols above or below the existing chord symbols, being sure to account for mutations. That's all there is to it — your harmony is transposed.

If you are being called upon to transpose the melody, you may either write a "lead sheet" or do it by ear. Though you may eventually develop the ability to transpose melody <u>and</u> harmony by ear, you will still find it helpful to think in terms of figured bass.

MODULATION

Modulation is the process of changing from one key to another within a song. Whether analyzing, composing, arranging or improvising, sooner or later you are going to want to understand modulation.

Modulation commonly occurs through the use of one or more <u>pivot chords</u> or a <u>jump-cut</u>.

A pivot chord is a chord that belongs to both keys (the key you are in, and the key you are modulating to), but has a different harmonic function in each. For example, a G major chord functions as the tonic triad in the key of G major, and the dominant triad in the key of C major. When you want to use a pivot chord (or pivot chords) to modulate, simply look for one or more chords which are common to both the key you are in, and the key you plan to go to. As you write or play this chord (or chords), begin thinking in terms of the figured bass of the new key. Your ears (and any other listener's ears) will then readily adjust to the new key.

A jump-cut happens much more suddenly. To execute a jump-cut, simply "cut" into the new key by "jumping" to one of it's chords. Obviously, it is sometimes more difficult to be graceful when executing a jump-cut modulation.

When either type of modulation occurs, a musician may stay in the new key for the remainder of the song, return to the old key immediately, or anything in between. Often a modulation will lead into yet another modulation.

To more fully understand modulation, you will find it helpful to study written examples. Modulations are easy to spot. Look for any deviation from standard figured bass (i.e. mutations), accidentals written in a harmony, or a change in key signature. Any one of these occurrences indicates modulation is taking place or, in the case of a jump-cut, already has taken place!

In the following example, the F#m7 is functioning as a pivot chord. This pivot chord's first appearance takes us from the key of E major to the key of D major. Its second appearance takes us from the key of D major back to the key of E major. Pretty slick!

continued:

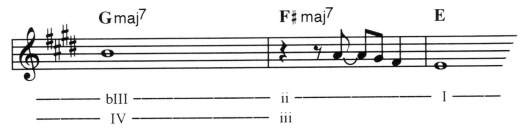

This next example makes use of a jump-cut (the A7 chord) to get us from the key of F major to the key of D minor. This example also contains a pivot chord (the Dm chord) which transports us from the key of D minor to the key of C major. Finally, C major's V chord (G7) is mutated to v (Gm7), thereby jump-cutting us back to the key of F major. Super slick!

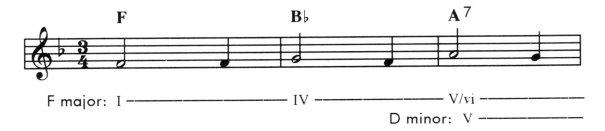

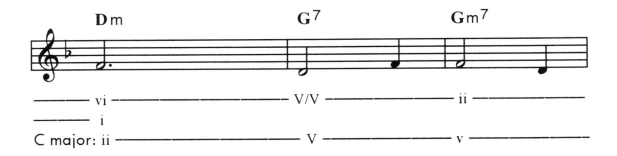

The following example uses a descending chromatic line as the rationale for a series of jump-cut modulations.

Db major: I ————————————————————— ii —————————————————

Eb major: IV ————————————————————— I —————————————————

D major: IV ————————————————————— iii —————————————————

F major: I ——————————— D major: V ————— v —————————————

Db major: bVII ———————————— V ——— V ————————— I ———

Some modulations use a diminished chord to destroy the tonality (i.e. pitch center) of the old key before jump-cutting to the new key. Because the diminished chord is not a member of the standard figured bass of either key, it assumes the role of a harmonic arbitrator — a sort of "inside-out pivot chord". This type of modulation makes use of aspects which are characteristic of both pivot chord modulation and jump-cut modulation. Musicians old saying: "Hit a diminished chord and go anywhere!"

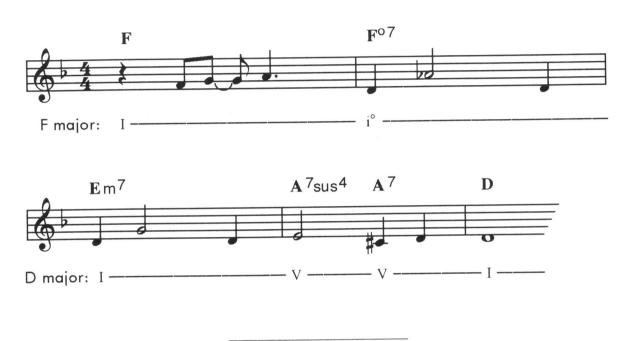

MUSIC CONSTRUCTION

The most effective way to learn how music is put together is to put together some music — compose! First, learn how to write a melody. Then learn how to add a harmony to your melody. Finally, learn how to "stretch out" your harmonized melody to form a complete composition. Here goes!

CREATING MELODY

There are as many ways to write a melody as there are people who write melodies. What I will show you is a foolproof way to write a melody. You may use this method any time, and especially during your moments of minimal inspiration. Sit down at your piano with a pencil and some blank music paper. Draw a treble clef. Close your eyes. With your right hand strike a single note. Open your eyes to see which note you have chosen.

After you have decided how many beats you would like this first note to last, write it beside the treble clef, being careful to leave enough space for an as yet undetermined key signature and time signature. Now, set everything down while you learn about motives.

A motive is a melodic idea. It consists of a melodic question and a melodic answer. A melodic question is simply one or more melody notes which sound like they are headed somewhere and they haven't gotten there yet. A melodic answer is simply one or more melody notes which sound like a response to the melodic question. A melodic answer may take the form of another melodic question, or it may take the form of a final response to a melodic question. While motives vary in length, a typical motive is four measures: two measures of melodic question followed by two measures of melodic answer. You have already begun writing a typical motive. Now, let's get back to it.

Play your first note. In your mind's ear, listen for a following note which sounds acceptable to you. (If you don't hear one, the same note or any note close by will do.) Find this second note on the piano keyboard. After you have decided how many beats you would like this second note to last, write it beside your first note. If you don't already have two measures of melody, find a third note. Play your first two notes in rhythm. In your mind's ear, listen for a following note which sounds acceptable to you. (If you don't hear one, the same note or any note close by will do.) Find this third note on the piano keyboard. After you have decided how many beats you would like this third note to last, write it beside your first two notes. Keep repeating this process until you have a group of melody notes which can be construed as two measures. Write the bar lines where they belong. Then write the time signature where it belongs. Congratulations! You have written a melodic question!

Now, with the mental strength you have left, write a melodic answer. Find the first note of your melodic answer by playing your melodic question, listening for a following note which sounds acceptable to you, etc. By now, your mind's ear is probably hearing the next two or three melody notes. If not, don't be concerned — just follow the process until you have a two measure melodic answer.

Now play the entire motive in rhythm. If the last note leaves you with a feeling that the melody wants to continue, your melodic answer has taken the form of another melodic question. If the last note leaves you with a feeling that the melody has ended, your melodic answer has taken the form of a final response, and you will want to change the last note so that your melodic answer takes the form of another melodic question. This is done so that your motive can be stretched out into a theme.

A theme is two consecutive motives. So a typical theme is eight measures in length. It usually follows this format: a two measure melodic question, followed by a two measure melodic answer which takes the form of another melodic question, followed by a two measure melodic question, followed by a two measure melodic answer which takes the form of a final response. A theme's format could be abbreviated to look like this: ? ? ? .

A typical theme is identical in form to this common household conversation:

FATHER: "Son, will you take out the garbage?"

SON: "Aw Dad, why do I always have to take out the garbage?"

FATHER: "Do I have to ask you again?"

SON: "I'll take it out."

So a typical theme is three questions followed by a final response.
Go ahead and stretch your motive into a theme. If you have any problem getting your final response to sound final, use tonic for your last note. (Yes, by now, based on the notes you have chosen, you should be capable of determining the key your melody is in.)

If you are dissatisfied with the sound of your newly composed theme, consider two things: 1.) You can always write another.
    2.) The harmony you add will greatly enhance the sound of your theme.

Here is an example:

THEME # 1

Notice that because I began with a "pick-up" note, the questions don't end at a bar line.

Here is another example:

THEME #2

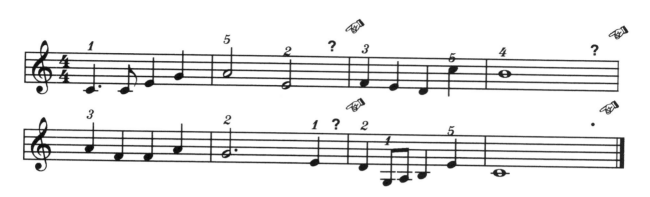

BUILDING HARMONY

There are as many ways to write a harmony as there are people who write harmonies. What I will show you is two foolproof ways to write a harmony. You may harmonize your theme by note or by chord symbol. It will be to your advantage to understand both ways.

"AS WRITTEN" HARMONIZATION

Begin by writing your theme on a grand staff. At the bottom of your music paper, on a separate grand staff, write the notes to the chords which occur in the key that your theme is written in. For example, if your theme is in the key of D, this separate grand staff would look like this:

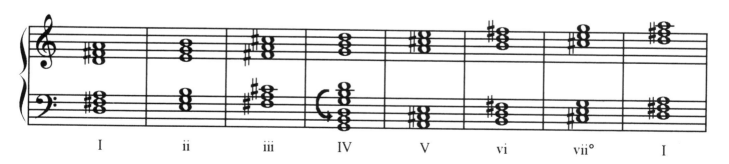

I   ii   iii   IV   V   vi   vii°   I

Now all you have to do is figure out which chords fit with which melody notes. For simplicity's sake, on this first harmonization, plan on using one chord per measure. Determine which note or notes occupy at least one half of the total number of beats in the first measure of your theme. This is easily done if your first measure looks like this:

The note B takes up two of the measure's three beats, so the note B is the "at least one half" we are looking for. You would now go down to the grand staff at the bottom of your music paper to find all the chords which contain the note B. Then, in pencil, you would write the figured bass symbols of those chords which contain a B, in no particular order, under the first measure of your theme.

If your first measure looks more like this:

then several "at least one half" situations exist. The notes F# and C# together represent at least one half of the measure; the notes C# and D together represent at least one half of the measure; and the notes F# and D together represent at least one half of the measure. You would go down to the grand staff at the bottom of your music paper to find all the chords which contain both F# and C# together; then C# and D together; and then F# and D together. Then, in pencil, you would write the figured bass symbols of these chords, in no particular order, under the first measure of your theme.

Follow this process through each measure of your theme.

Using Theme #1 as an example:

Using Theme #2 as an example:

The figured bass symbols represent chords which will fit (i.e. sound acceptable) with a particular measure.

To decide on one chord per measure, you may either arbitrarily choose one of these figured bass symbols per measure or you may listen to the sound of each chord being held down while all of a measure's melody notes are being played. Either way, you will want to erase the unchosen figured bass symbols so that only one symbol per measure remains.

When you have decided on one figured bass symbol per measure, all that remains to be done is the actual arrangement of harmony notes. You may use solid chords (all chord members struck simultaneously), broken chords (chord members struck one at a time), partial chords, rests, and anything else your devious mind comes up with. Feel free to write harmony notes in the treble clef, under your melody. (Any harmony note placed above the melody will cease to function like a harmony note because it will replace the melody. For now, the melody must be the highest note. Descant voicing will be covered in chapter ten.) To give you an idea of what your "as written" harmonization might look like and how it might sound, here is Theme #1 with one of its possible accompaniments:

Here is Theme #2 with one of its possible accompaniments:

"CHORD SYMBOL" HARMONIZATION

To harmonize your theme by chord symbol is a lot less work. Begin by writing your theme on music paper. At the bottom of your music paper write the standard figured bass symbols. Above each figured bass symbol write the corresponding chord symbol which occurs in the key that your theme is written. For example, if your theme is in the key of D major, you would write this:

D	Em	F#m	G	A	Bm	C#dim
I	ii	iii	IV	V	vi	vii°

Now all you have to do is figure out which chord symbols fit with which melody notes. For simplicity's sake, on this first harmonization, plan on using one chord symbol per measure. Using the "trial and error" method, listen to the sound of each chord being held down while all of a measure's melody notes are being played. If more than one chord sounds acceptable, choose the one which appeals to you the most. When you have written one chord symbol above each measure, you are done. Using any chord symbol approach, the actual arrangement of harmony notes is done spontaneously, so no written arrangement of harmony notes is necessary!

To give you an idea of what your "chord symbol" harmonization might look like, here is Theme #1 with one of its possible accompaniments:

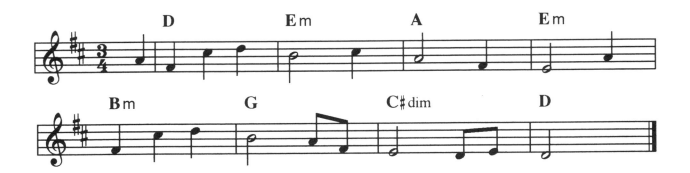

Here is Theme #2 with one of its possible accompaniments:

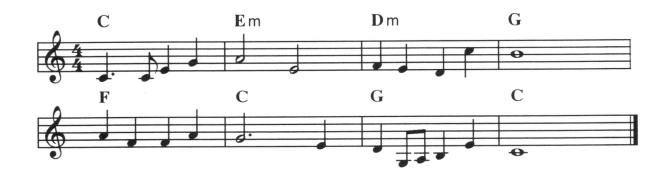

SONGFORM

The first theme of a song is labeled the "A theme". The second theme of a song is labeled the "B theme". If there is a third theme, it is labeled the "C theme", and so on. When a theme is repeated, but with a slight change in the melody and/or harmony and/or rhythm, it is labeled "A' theme" (pronounced "A prime theme") or "B' theme", etc. The term "songform" refers to the arrangement of themes. A typical songform is: A A' B A. Other common songforms are: A A' B, A B A, A B A B, and A B A C A.

The B theme is musical material relevant to the A theme. It is also a pleasant departure from the A theme. Even though the A theme is the first main theme presented in a piece of music, the B theme is more often remembered by the listener. This is because the A theme is typically used to "build up" to the B theme. In typical songform, A and A' equate to your working all year so that you may take that magnificent (B theme) vacation before you go back to (A theme) work.

You may now stretch your harmonized theme out into an entire song using any songform you like.

Note: If you choose to study the songform of some of your favorite songs, you should be aware of the fact that some portions of many songs cannot be construed as part of a theme. Measures included in this category are:

the "introduction": several measures which lead into the (A) theme, used to set the mood of the song.

the "interlude" or the "bridge": several measures used to connect two themes.

the "coda": several measures used to bring the song to an end.

DEVELOPMENT

Development is the process of changing melody, harmony or rhythm. For example, a theme may be shortened, lengthened, broken up into smaller sections, have a section or sections repeated higher or lower, have its notes grouped differently, have its harmony and/or rhythm changed, etc.

In serious music (also called "classical music"), development is used to stretch motifs (motives) and subjects (themes) out into extended musical works. In popular music, development is used less often. However, development is a basic procedure of improvisation (composing music at the same time it is being performed) and many popular songs contain improvisation.

You will find more specific information about development in chapters eight, nine and ten.

A SALES PITCH ABOUT CONSTRUCTING YOUR OWN MUSIC

The best way to learn how a <u>house</u> is put together is to actually build one, using your mind, two hands, some simple tools, the necessary materials and lots of sweat. To experience the thought processes necessary for sound construction; to work blisters into calluses; to learn how to make simple tools perform complex tasks; to join materials into one magnificent whole; to labor so hard that when you finally stop, you feel the blood course through your veins — the joy that is experienced is equaled only by the intensity with which you apply yourself to the great challenge. You are developing an understanding of construction which cannot be obtained from books. You are kindling respect for yourself and for all that is involved. While other people share in the joy of the "do-it-yourselfer", only you receive the profound learning experience and the intense satisfaction of accomplishment. The home you have created becomes, undeniably, a part of you.

The best way to learn how a <u>song</u> is put together is to actually write one, using your mind, two hands, some simple tools, the necessary materials and a little sweat. To experience the thought processes necessary for sound melodic, harmonic and rhythmic construction; to work blisters into calluses; to learn how to make simple tools perform complex tasks; to join materials into one magnificent whole; to concentrate so long that when you finally stop, you feel the blood course through your brain — the joy that is experienced is equaled only by the intensity with which you apply yourself to the great challenge. You are developing an understanding of melodic, harmonic and rhythmic construction which cannot be obtained from books. You are kindling respect for yourself and for all that is involved. While other people share in the joy of the "do-it-yourselfer", only you receive the profound learning experience and the intense satisfaction of accomplishment. The music you have created becomes, undeniably, a part of you.

You may live all your life happily, in houses someone else built. You may live all your life happily, playing music someone else wrote. Until you build your own home, you have experienced only a fraction of what a home has to offer. Until you write your own music, you have experienced only a fraction of what music has to offer.

CHAPTER SEVEN
INTERMEDIATE EAR

In this chapter you will learn the basics of how to actually begin playing by ear. But don't get excited. You're not done honing the holes on either side of your head. There's still a small amount of ear training left to learn before we start the "play by ear" process.

LOWERED INTERVALS

Learn to hear the difference among the five lowered intervals found in chapter six. Each interval has its own unique sound:

m2nd – sounds like a buzz
m3rd – sounds like the beginning of a funeral march
dim5th – sounds like a hollowed out diminished chord
m6th – sounds like a hollowed out augmented chord
m7th – sounds like it wants to resolve (i.e. move on to other notes)

Play these and listen to them. To get to the point where you are able to consistently hear the difference among them, you will have to get someone else to play them for you. This will allow you to sit across the room, look the other way and identify each interval solely by sound.

When you are able to aurally identify each randomly-played interval (eight out of ten is okay for starters), move on to the three common seventh chords found in chapter six.

THREE COMMON SEVENTH CHORDS

The easiest way to learn how to aurally distinguish among the three common seventh chords is to listen for the overall quality. The dominant seventh chord, being a chord of action, sounds like it wants to resolve (i.e. move on to another chord). The major seventh chord, being a chord of repose, sounds like it wants to stay right where it is. The minor seventh chord commonly functions either way — as a chord of action or as a chord of repose. Consequently, it sounds like it can't decide whether it wants to resolve or stay right where it is.

When you are able to aurally identify each randomly-played chord (eight out of ten is okay for starters), you are done!

PLAYING BY EAR

Any music you learn to play by ear is known as your "arrangement" of that music. Initially, your arrangement will be figured out in this order:

> 1.) melody notes
> 2.) bass line notes
> 3.) harmony notes

The melody notes of any song are easily recognized as the highest and/or most prominent notes. The bass line notes of any song are recognized as the absolute lowest notes. All harmony notes are usually located under the melody notes and always above the bass line notes. (The only time the melody will not be the highest notes is when a descant line [or lines] is included by the composer or arranger. Descant lines usually occur way above the melody, are often played by violins, and are easily discernible from the melody notes. Do not include any descant lines in your piano arrangement unless 1.) there is a break in the melody allowing you to do so, or 2.) you don't mind leaving out the bass line, or 3.) the bass line is the melody, or 4.) you have three hands.) The melody, being (usually) the highest notes, and the bass line, being the lowest notes, are known collectively as "outer voices". Except for descant lines, harmony notes are always sandwiched between the melody and the bass line, and are referred to collectively as "inner voices". Initially, outer voices are much easier to hear. They also provide clues which help to figure out the inner voices. This is why you must, at least initially, work on figuring out only the melody notes, then only the bass line notes and finally the harmony notes. To do it in any other order, or in combination, will result in your becoming discouraged.

Begin by recording any song you enjoy listening to, and which you don't have in written form. (Use a cassette recorder because it is mobile and convenient.) Take your cassette recorder over to your piano and have a seat. Press the play button and wait till you hear the very first melody note of your chosen song. Then immediately shut the cassette player off. Hum, whistle or bark this first note while finding the note which is identical in pitch on the piano keyboard. (This is called "pitch matching".) This done, rewind your cassette, press play and wait till you hear the first two notes. Immediately shut the cassette player off.

Hum, whistle or bark the first two notes. Determine which interval you are hearing, then play these first two notes on the piano keyboard. This done, rewind your cassette, press play and wait till you hear the first three notes, etc. If you should come upon a melody note that you can't readily find on the piano keyboard, skip it, go on to the next note or two, then come back to it. Doing this will allow you to "back up" to the note, possibly making it more detectable. So, when discerning any particular melody note, you have three angles of attack: 1.) pitch match, 2.) determine the intervallic relationship between the note you are attempting to figure out and the note which comes before it, or 3.) determine the intervallic relationship between the note you are attempting to figure out and the note which comes after it. As you get better, you will notice yourself figuring out two and three melody notes at a time.

When figuring out the melody of a song by ear, it sometimes helps, at least initially, to write down the note heads on a piece of music paper. If you choose to do this, don't feel that it's necessary to indicate note values — you will find that written note heads are sufficient.

When you have figured out the entire melody, begin figuring out the bass line notes. Because the bass line is made up of notes played one at a time, you may use the same process you used to figure out the melody notes. However, because the bass line is buried underneath the harmony and melody, it is not as easily discerned.

When figuring out the bass line of a song by ear, it sometimes helps, at least initially, to write down the letter names of the bass line notes, above the melody note heads, on a piece of music paper. These letter names may be stretched out into chord symbols when the harmony is figured out.

By now you should be able to determine which key you are in. Write out the standard figured bass and the corresponding chord symbols for reference use when figuring out the harmony.

When you have the entire bass line, begin figuring out the harmony. When figuring out the harmony, you have two clues with which to work. Clue #1 is the bass line notes. Almost always, the bass line consists of at least the root and/or the fifth of the chord you are attempting to discern. This being the case, Clue #1 will generally tell you the letter name of the chord in question. Clue #2 is the melody notes.

Almost always, the melody will contain several notes for each bass line note that occurs. When this is the case, look through the melody notes to help you find out what type of chord (major, minor, diminished, etc.) you are dealing with. You will undoubtedly find the instance where you have but one melody note for one bass line note. When this is the case, unless the melody note is identical to the bass line note, you will have two chord members with which to figure out the chord you are discerning. For example, if your bass line note is C and your melody note is Eb, you are probably dealing with either a C minor chord or a C diminished chord. So, Clue #2 will generally lead you to the type of chord in question.

In the rare instance that Clue #1 and/or Clue #2 don't provide enough assistance, you can always revert back to the skills acquired through your ear training. In other words, to determine which chord you are dealing with, listen to the overall quality of the chord in question. If a final, last-gasp effort is necessary, use the "trial and error" method (using the standard figured bass and corresponding chord symbol chart) to determine the correct harmony. Note: Mutations are commonplace and cannot be discerned using the standard figured bass and corresponding chord symbol chart. When mutations occur, you must be able to rely on Clue #1 and/or Clue #2 and/or the skills acquired through your ear training.

If you have trouble figuring out the melody of a particular song by ear, go on to another song. If you still have trouble, either 1.) you are choosing very fast melodies, which make it difficult to discern individual notes, or 2.) you need more work on your intervallic ear training, or 3.) you need a preparatory exercise. No problem. Here it is:

Record yourself, or someone else, playing the melody of several songs you have not previously practiced. Figure out these melodies by ear, following the process described earlier. Being that you won't have the distraction of a harmony or a bass line, you should find this much easier to do.

If you are able to figure out the melodies of songs by ear, but have trouble discerning bass line notes, then record yourself, or someone else, playing the bass line of several songs you have not previously practiced. Figure out these bass lines by ear, following the process described earlier. Being that you won't have the distraction of a harmony or a melody, you should find this much easier to do.

If you have trouble figuring out the harmony of the songs you are playing by ear, it is probably because you are attempting to be precise. Especially when it comes to harmony, close counts! At times, when I was learning how to play by ear, I went to great lengths to figure out the exact chord, only to change it in my final arrangement because I found another chord which I thought sounded better. Using your knowledge of figured bass and replacement chords, you will be exact or very close when figuring out harmonies by ear. Keep two things in mind:

1.) This is your arrangement of someone else's music. You are free to change, add or delete virtually anything. Respect yourself and your preferences at least as much as the original composer and his intentions. (Remember who owns your piano.)

2.) You will get better with each arrangement you make. The transference of knowledge which takes place (from one piece to another) when playing by ear is much greater than the transference of knowledge which takes place during "as written" or "chord symbol" performance. If your first arrangements are a little rough or slightly inaccurate, so what? You will get better quickly. You may then come back and "tighten up" any loose arrangements.

As you continue to make arrangements by ear, you will find yourself creating short cuts. You will begin to figure out the harmony and the melody simultaneously, hence, the amount of time it takes you to make an arrangement will decrease. Your goal as an ear musician is to continually reduce the amount of time it takes you to make an arrangement. eventually, you will be able to create an arrangement "on the spot" after hearing a song once or twice. To do this, you must become capable of "analytic listening" — that is, you must become capable of hearing and remembering the songform and the chord progression in terms of figured bass. Analytic listening abilities are developed only through the experience of comparing what is heard with what is played by ear, over and over again, through many different arrangements, until you, the ear musician, say something like: "Here's another A A' B A songform..."or: "This song is basically just I, vi, ii, V, I, except for the deceptive cadence in the B theme."

Now, I wish to reiterate: At least initially, when playing by ear, choose songs which you really like, but which you don't have in written form. The more you like the song, the more likely you are to go through the entire "play by ear" process. Also, the easier it will be for you because you will be able to relate or identify more closely with the music. Your mind will be easily drawn to the music.

One final observation for those of you who happen to choose fast songs to "rip by ear": listen to a 33 1/3 RPM record playing at 16 RPM. The fast music you are attempting to play by ear will be slowed to half of the original speed, will remain in the same key, and will be heard one octave lower. Use of this technique is also possible with a two-speed reel-to-reel tape recorder or a two-speed cassette. The advantages are obvious. Both my students and I have used this technique to tame many wild jazz improvisations. Have fun!

CHAPTER EIGHT
ADVANCED THEORY

I've heard it said that obtaining quality is a lot like buying oats. If you want nice, clean, fresh oats, you must pay a fair price. However, if you can be satisfied with oats that have already been through the horse, that comes a little cheaper. Likewise, to obtain a quality sound on the piano, you must pay a fair price. This chapter represents a large portion of that cost. If you read it very carefully the first time through, you won't have to "pay it again, Sam".

VOICING

Voicing is a term used to describe the way you choose to arrange the notes of a particular chord. During Two Hand Method performance, you voiced your chords in root position. During Three Hand Method performance, you voiced your chords in whatever position was necessary to allow your right hand to reach the melody notes. In both methods, the systems I taught you dictated your chord voicings for you. With Arpeggiation Method, you gained a little more freedom in voicing your chords.

Chord voicing is an integral part of Chord Scale Improvisation, Non-Harmonic Tone Improvisation, and Jazz/Modal Improvisation. Throughout chapters eight, nine and ten, you will be provided with the information necessary to understand the thought processes which should take place when you voice chords.

CHORD SCALES

Until now, we have considered chords and scales as separate entities. However, essentially, chords and scales are the same thing. Does this sound impossible? Read on...

Tertian harmony is harmony made up of thirds. 99.9% of all the music you will ever play or hear is comprised of tertian harmony. The other .1% is either secundal harmony (made up of seconds) or quartal harmony (made up of fourths).

Here is how tertian harmony is built on the note C:

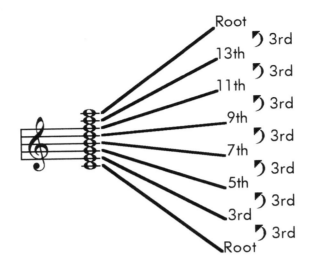

Because this is as large as a C chord gets, we call this configuration of notes the "C grand chord".

When we bring the 9th, 11th, 13th and root down one octave, we get this:

Now let's compare the C grand chord to the C scale:

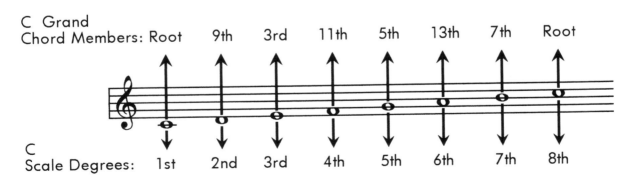

Notice that every note that is in the C grand chord is also in the C scale. Essentially, the C grand chord is the C scale. This concept holds true over the entire keyboard — any chord can be thought of as a scale and any scale can be thought of as a chord.

If there is any difference between chords and scales, it lies in our use of the terms "chord" and "scale". The term "chord" implies vertical stacking of notes, indicative of harmony:

The term "scale" implies horizontal movement of notes, indicative of melody:

However, harmonies commonly consist of horizontal movement:

And melodies commonly overlap with one another, making use of vertical stacking:

So, while there is an implied difference between the terms "chord" and "scale", no such difference exists, all the time, in actuality.

SPECIAL INSTRUCTION CHORDS

In chapter six, you discovered the ten common special instruction chords. I used C as an example, and they looked like this:

Csus	also written as: Csus4
C6	
Cm6	
C7sus	also written as: C7sus4
C7(#5)	also written as: C7(+5) or C7+
C7(b5)	also written as: C7(-5)
Cm7(b5)	also written as: CØ7
C°7	also written as: Cdim7
Cm(#7)	also written as: Cm(+7)
C/D	also written as: C/D bass or $\frac{C}{D}$

I also mentioned the one special instruction which is not a chord:

N.C.	also written as: No Chord

Using C as an example, here are the remaining special instruction chords of any practical consequence:

C9	
C(add9)	also written as: C(add2)
C(b9)	also written as: C(-9)
C(#9)	also written as: C(+9)
C9(#5)	also written as: C9(+5) or C+9
C9(b5)	also written as: C9(-5)
C6/9	also written as: C6(add9)
C9 (no5)	
C9 (no3)	
Cm(add9)	also written as: Cm(add2)
Cm(b9)	also written as: Cm(-9)
C7(b9)	also written as: C7(-9)
C7(#9)	also written as: C7(+9)
Cmaj9	
Cmaj7(b9)	also written as: Cmaj7(-9)

Cmaj7(#9)   also written as: Cmaj7(+9)
Cm7(b9)   also written as: Cm7(-9)
C11
C11(b9)   also written as: C11(-9)
C11(#9)   also written as: C11(+9)
Cm11
Cmaj11
C(#11)   also written as: C(+11)
Cm(#11)   also written as: Cm(+11)
C7(#11)   also written as: C7(+11)
Cmaj7(#11) also written as: Cmaj7(+11)
Cm7(#11)   also written as: Cm7(+11)
C9(#11)   also written as: C9(+11)
Cmaj9(#11) also written as: Cmaj9(+11)
Cm9(#11)   also written as: Cm9(+11)
C(b9#11)   also written as: C(-9+11)
C(#9#11)   also written as: C(+9+11)
C13
Cm13
Cmaj13
C13(b9)   also written as: C13(-9)
C13(b5b9)   also written as: C13(-5-9)
Cm13(b9)   also written as: Cm13(-9)
Cmaj13(b9) also written as: Cmaj13(-9)
C13(#9)   also written as: C13(+9)
Cmaj13(#9) also written as: Cmaj13(+9)
C13(#11)   also written as: C13(+11)
Cmaj13(#11) also written as: Cmaj13(+11)
Cm13(#11)   also written as: Cm13(+11)
C13(#9#11) also written as: C13(+9+11)

Don't be intimidated by this list — with the exception of jazz and contemporary gospel, these chords occur infrequently. Whenever any of these less-common special instruction chords present themselves in your music, just focus your attention on them beforehand, so you'll be prepared.

Now let's cover each of these chords individually:

The C9 chord is a C7 chord with the 9th tacked on top. The notes in this chord are C, E, G, Bb and D. This five note chord may demand that your right hand stretch further than it's able. Also, this five note chord may occasionally create more of a full chord sound than desired. You may handle either of these two situations by leaving out certain chord members. To know which chord members are most appropriately left out, you must understand the relative importance of each:

9th   – very important; adds harmonic color
7th   – very important; adds harmonic color
5th   – least important; adds bulk without adding much harmonic color
3rd   – very important; adds harmonic color
Root – unimportant; adds bulk without adding much harmonic color

The 3rd, 7th and 9th provide all the harmonic color necessary for any 9th chord to function as a 9th chord. As such, the 3rd, 7th and 9th are referred to as the "strong chord members". Except for some types of jazz/modal improvisation, all your chord symbol performance will include (at least) the root and the 5th in the left hand. This being the case, your right hand should not harbor any guilt feelings about leaving out these two chord members. So, whenever it is either impossible, inconvenient or undesirable to include all the chord members of a 9th chord, feel perfectly free to leave out the root and/or the 5th in the right hand voicing.

C(add9) is, quite obviously, a C chord with the 9th added. The notes in this chord are C, E, G and D. Frequently, this chord is voiced with the 9th between the root and the 3rd: C, D, E, G. This makes the chord more accessible to people with normal-size hands. Again, the root and/or the 5th may be left out of the right hand voicing because the 3rd and the 9th are the strong chord members.

C(b9) is a C chord with a flatted 9th added. The notes in this chord are C, E, G and Db. The 3rd and the flatted 9th are the strong chord members.

C(#9) is a C chord with a sharped 9th added. The notes in this chord are C, E, G and D#. The 3rd and the sharped 9th are the strong chord members.

C9(#5) is a C9 chord with a sharped 5th. The notes in this chord are C, E, G#, Bb and D. The 3rd, sharped 5th, 7th and 9th are the strong chord members.

C9(b5) is a C9 chord with a flatted 5th. The notes in this chord are C, E, Gb, Bb and D. The 3rd, flatted 5th, 7th and 9th are the strong chord members

C6/9 is a C chord with the 6th and the 9th added. The notes in this chord are C, E, G, A and D. The 3rd, 6th and 9th are the strong chord members.

C9(no5) is a C9 chord with the 5th left out. The notes in this chord are C, E, Bb and D. The 3rd, 7th and 9th are the strong chord members.

C9(no3) is a C9 chord with the 3rd left out. The notes in this chord are C, G, Bb and D. The 7th and the 9th are the strong chord members.

Cm9 is a Cm7 chord with the 9th added. The notes in this chord are C, Eb, G, Bb and D. The 3rd, 7th and 9th are the strong chord members.

Cm(add9) is a Cm chord with the 9th added. The notes in this chord are C, Eb, G and D. Frequently, this chord is voiced with the 9th between the root and the 3rd: C, D, Eb, G. The 3rd and the 9th are the strong chord members.

Cm(b9) is a Cm chord with a flatted 9th added. The notes in this chord are C, Eb, G and Db. The 3rd and the flatted 9th are the strong chord members.

C7(b9) is a C7 chord with a flatted 9th added. The notes in this chord are C, E, G, Bb and Db. The 3rd, 7th and flatted 9th are the strong chord members.

C7(#9) is a C7 chord with a sharped 9th added. The notes in this chord are C, E, G, Bb and D#. The 3rd, 7th and sharped 9th are the strong chord members.

Cmaj9 is a Cmaj7 chord with the 9th added. The notes in this chord are C, E, G, B and D. The 3rd, 7th and 9th are the strong chord members.

Cmaj7(b9) is a Cmaj7 chord with a flatted 9th added. The notes in this chord are C, E, G, B and Db. The 3rd, 7th and flatted 9th are the strong chord members.

Cmaj7(#9) is a Cmaj7 chord with a sharped 9th added. The notes in this chord are C, E, G, B and D#. The 3rd, 7th and sharped 9th are the strong chord members.

Cm7(b9) is a Cm7 chord with a flatted 9th added. The notes in this chord are C, Eb, G, Bb and Db. The 3rd, 7th and flatted 9th are the strong chord members.

C11 is a C9 chord with the 11th added. The notes in this chord are C, E, G, Bb, D and F. The 3rd, 7th and 11th are the strong chord members.

C11(b9) is a C11 chord with a flatted 9th. The notes in this chord are C, E, G, Bb, Db and F. The 3rd, 7th, flatted 9th and 11th are the strong chord members.

C11(#9) is a C11 chord with a sharped 9th. The notes in this chord are C, E, G, Bb, D# and F. The 3rd, 7th, sharped 9th and 11th are the strong chord members.

Cm11 is a Cm9 chord with the 11th added. The notes in this chord are C, Eb, G, Bb, D and F. The 3rd, 7th and 11th are the strong chord members.

Cmaj11 is a Cmaj9 chord with the 11th added. The notes in this chord are C, E, G, B, D and F. The 3rd, 7th and 11th are the strong chord mernbers.

C(#11) is a C chord with a sharped 11th added. The notes in this chord are C, E, G and F#. The 3rd and the sharped 11th are the strong chord members.

Cm(#11) is a Cm chord with a sharped 11th added. The notes in this chord are C, Eb, G and F#. The 3rd and the sharped 11th are the strong chord members.

C7(#11) is a C7 chord with a sharped 11th added. The notes in this chord are C, E, G, Bb and F#. The 3rd, 7th and sharped 11th are the strong chord members.

Cmaj7(#11) is a Cmaj7 chord with a sharped 11th added. The notes in this chord are C, E, G, B and F#. The 3rd, 7th and sharped 11th are the strong chord members.

Cm7(#11) is a Cm7 chord with a sharped 11th added. The notes in this chord are C, Eb, G, Bb and F#. The 3rd, 7th and sharped 11th are the strong chord members.

C9(#11) is a C9 chord with a sharped 11th added. The notes in this chord are C, E, G, Bb, D and F#. The 3rd, 7th, 9th and sharped 11th are the strong chord members.

Cmaj9(#11) is a Cmaj9 chord with a sharped 11th added. The notes in this chord are C, E, G, B, D and F#. The 3rd, 7th, 9th and sharped 11th are the strong chord members.

Cm9(#11) is a Cm9 chord with a sharped 11th added. The notes in this chord are C, Eb, G, Bb, D and F#. The 3rd, 7th, 9th and sharped 11th are the strong chord members.

C(b9#11) is a C chord with a flatted 9th and a sharped 11th added. The notes in this chord are C, E, G, Db and F#. The 3rd, flatted 9th and sharped 11th are the strong chord members.

C(#9#11) is a C chord with a sharped 9th and a sharped 11th added The notes in this chord are C, E, G, D# and F#. The 3rd, sharped 9th and sharped 11th are the strong chord members.

C13 is a C11 chord with the 13th added. The notes in this chord are C, E, G, Bb, D, F and A. The 3rd, 7th and 13th are the strong chord members. Frequently, this chord is voiced with the 3rd between the 7th and the 13th: Bb, E, A

Cm13 is a Cm11 chord with the 13th added. The notes in this chord are C, Eb, G, Bb, D, F and A. The 3rd, 7th and 13th are the strong chord members. Frequently, this chord is voiced with the 3rd between the 7th and the 13th: Bb, Eb, A

Cmaj13 is a Cmaj11 chord with the 13th added. The notes in this chord are C, E, G, B, D, F and A. The 3rd, 7th and 13th are the strong chord members. Frequently, this chord is voiced with the 3rd between the 7th and the 13th: B, E, A

C13(b9) is a C13 chord with a flatted 9th. The notes in this chord are C, E, G, Bb, Db, F and A. The 3rd, 7th, flatted 9th and 13th are the strong chord members.

C13(b5b9) is a C13 chord with a flatted 5th and a flatted 9th. The notes in this chord are C, E, Gb, Bb, Db, F and A. The 3rd, flatted 5th, 7th, flatted 9th and 13th are the strong chord members.

Cmaj13(b9) is a Cm13 chord with a flatted 9th. The notes in this chord are C, Eb, G, Bb, Db, F and A. The 3rd, 7th, flatted 9th and 13th are the strong chord members.

Cmaj13(b9) is a Cmaj13 chord with a flatted 9th. The notes in this chord are C, E, G, B, Db, F and A. The 3rd,7th, flatted 9th and 13th are the strong chord members.

C13(#9) is a C13 chord with a sharped 9th. The notes in this chord are C, E, G, Bb, D#, F and A. The 3rd, 7th, sharped 9th and 13th are the strong chord members.

Cmaj13(#9) is a Cmaj13 chord with a sharped 9th. The notes in this chord are C, E, G, B, D#, F and A. The 3rd, 7th, sharped 9th and 13th are the strong chord members.

C13(#11) is a C13 chord with a sharped 11th. The notes in this chord are C, E, G, Bb, D, F# and A. The 3rd, 7th, sharped 11th and 13th are the strong chord members.

Cmaj13(#11) is a Cmaj13 chord with a sharped 11th. The notes in this chord are C, E, G, B, D, F# and A. The 3rd, 7th, sharped 11th and 13th are the strong chord members.

Cm13(#11) is a Cm13 chord with a sharped 11th. The notes in this chord are C, Eb, G, Bb, D, F# and A. The 3rd, 7th, sharped 11th and 13th are the strong chord members.

C13(#9#11) is a C13 chord with a sharped 9th and a sharped 11th. The notes in this chord are C, E, G, Bb, D#, F#, and A. The 3rd, 7th, sharped 9th, sharped 11th and 13th are the strong chord members.

If you live long enough, you just might run into some chord types other than those I have mentioned and which, by now, I'm sure you would be capable of figuring out. So, while there are other possible special instruction chords which could be built on the note C, any further explanation would be redundant.

When reading special instruction chords, you should understand the significance of the parenthesis. For example, let's compare these two chord symbols:

Cb9   C(b9)

Cb9 is built on the note Cb, and contains these notes: Cb, Eb, Gb, Bbb and Db.
C(b9) is built on the note C, and contains these notes: C, E, G and Db. <u>Without</u> the parenthesis, the flat sign refers to the letter C, telling us to play a Cb chord. <u>With</u> the parenthesis, the flat sign refers to the number 9, telling us to play a flatted 9th. This same principle holds true for these two:

C#11   C(#11)

C#11 is built on the note C#, and contains these notes: C#, E#, G#, B, D# and F#. C(#11) is built on the note C, and contains these notes: C, E, G and F#. <u>Without</u> the parenthesis, the sharp sign refers to the letter C, telling us to play a C# chord. <u>With</u> the parenthesis, the sharp sign refers to the number 11, telling us to play a sharped 11th.

One final point: Though melody notes may occasionally be heard as part of the harmony, when it comes to the written chord symbol, melody notes are not considered part of the harmony.

For example, let's look at the note Db in a C chord. When it functions as a member of the harmony, it should be mentioned in the chord symbol:

However, when it functions <u>only</u> as a member of the melody, it should not be mentioned in the chord symbol:

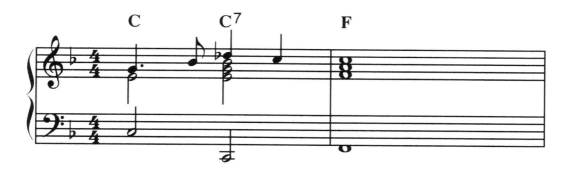

You will occasionally notice dim-wit ninny arrangers who include some melody notes in the chord symbol:

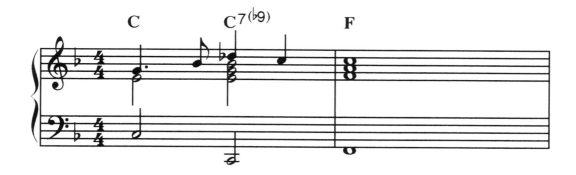

When this happens, chord symbol performers must decipher the unnecessary duplication — a small, slightly irritating inconvenience.

ALTERED TONES

When a chord member is raised one half step or lowered one half step, it is referred to as an "altered tone". Using a C chord as an example, let's look at all the possible altered tones which could occur in a major chord:

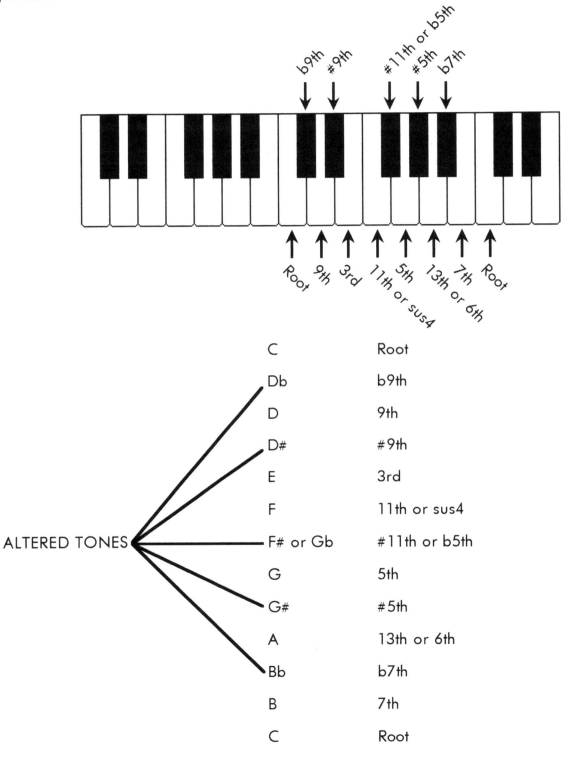

C	Root
Db	b9th
D	9th
D#	#9th
E	3rd
F	11th or sus4
F# or Gb	#11th or b5th
G	5th
G#	#5th
A	13th or 6th
Bb	b7th
B	7th
C	Root

ALTERED TONES

Now, using a Cm chord as an example, let's look at all the possible altered tones which could occur in a minor chord:

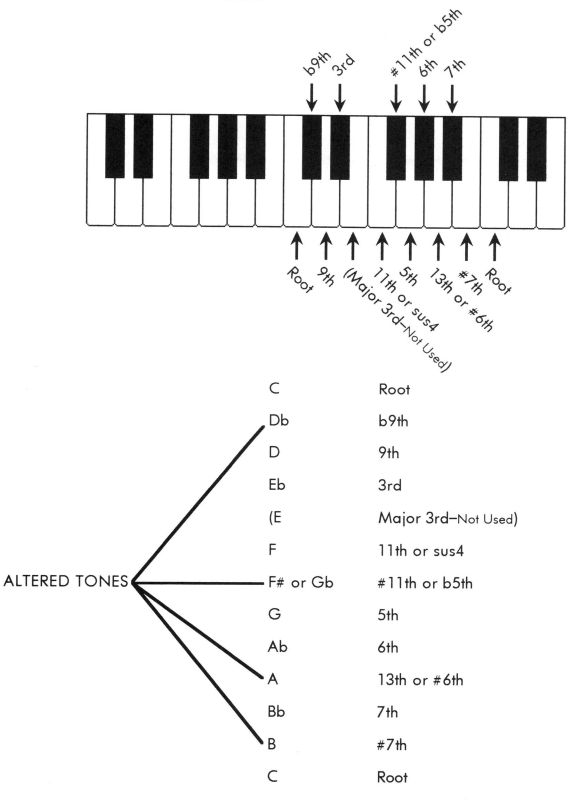

C	Root
Db	b9th
D	9th
Eb	3rd
(E	Major 3rd–Not Used)
F	11th or sus4
F# or Gb	#11th or b5th
G	5th
Ab	6th
A	13th or #6th
Bb	7th
B	#7th
C	Root

ALTERED TONES

Note: The Cm6 chord contains the notes C, Eb, G, and A, so it is actually making use of the #6th (characteristic of melodic minor), though the chord symbol itself does not relate this. The reason for this is that the Cm6 chord symbol was derived from the C6 chord (C, E, G, A), the only difference being the letter m, which refers to the lowered 3rd (C, <u>Eb</u>, G, A).

SCALE DEGREE PERSONALITIES

Chord members and altered tones may be collectively referred to as "scale degrees". Each scale degree has somewhat of a personality. Let's examine them individually:

The root, being the central note around which any chord is built, is "home" to all the other chord members and altered tones. The root functions as a mother to the chord. When you were a little baby chord builder, you always began your chords with the root. As you matured and went out into chord symbol land, the root became less important to your harmonic survival. So, like most mothers, it is occasionally left out.

The b9th scale degree is extremely dissonant. It may seem paradoxical that the strong dissonance created by the b9th results in some of music's most beautiful chords (provided resolution takes place). However, it is this dissonance, created by the b9th, which adds a great quantity of harmonic color to your music. To illustrate this point, listen to a b9th chord by itself:

Now listen to the same chord with a resolution:

The b9th chord by itself (i.e. out of context) is pain to most people's ears. Its ugliness abounds. The dissonance just hangs there, unresolved. The b9th chord with a resolution (i.e. in context) is tremendous harmonic beauty to most people's ears. The same dissonance exists, but the resolution handles it. This being the case, you must be very careful to have a place for the b9th chord to go (i.e. resolve).

The b9th scale degree is temperamental. It shares some of the same characteristics as the very small child who playfully strikes you and then, laughing, runs to the safety of his parent's arms. While this situation is often pleasant and memorable, it deserves to be handled carefully.

The 9th scale degree is very adaptable. It fits in almost anywhere, almost anytime. Generally, the 9th will add a plush quality to your major chords, and bring a pleasant quality of intrigue to your minor chords:

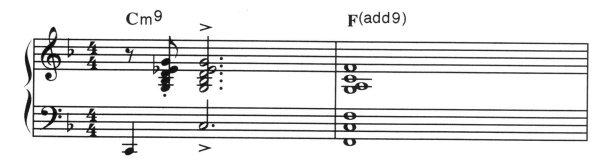

The 9th scale degree shares some of the same qualities of your best friend: almost always pleasant to have around; rarely bothersome.

The #9th scale degree is very dissonant, and yet, often this altered tone is left unresolved in jazz music. In fact, a type of jazz called "the blues" is based almost entirely on this #9th dissonance. In blues music, often the major 3rd (the note E in a C chord) is played at the same time as the #9th (the note D# in a C chord). Sometimes these scale degrees are spread out into a major 7th interval:

Other times they are played one half step apart:

While a real case of the blues may put a frown on a person's face, it has been my experience that blues music puts a smile on just about anyone's face. The #9th scale degree can be thought of as a "good-time Charlie" — include it in your music and you can be virtually certain your listeners (including yourself) will have a good time.

The b3rd scale degree (the 3rd of a minor chord) gives minor chords their characteristic sad sound:

This scale degree is often used to create gloom.

The 3rd scale degree is a very strong member of any chord. Because it helps preserve the rich harmonic color of virtually any chord, thereby guaranteeing a more full-bodied sound, this chord member can be thought of as a harmonic bodyguard.

The 11th (or sus4) scale degree will sometimes produce a "hanging" sound, like:

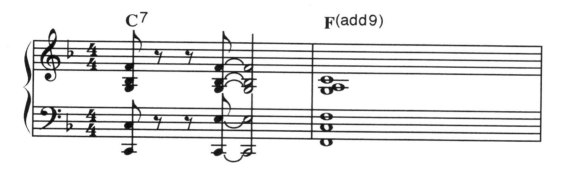

or:

However, this is not always the case:

Though it can be a very mellow addition to any harmony or melody, it has the potential of being very dissonant. The 11th (or sus4) scale degree is a lot like a co-worker who has occasional temper flare-ups — you have to know when to "step lightly" or else you could find yourself in trouble.

The #11th (or b5th) scale degree has a yearning quality, like:

or:

It is used a lot in all types of jazz:

The 5th scale degree is usually the least significant chord member. When played with the root, the result is a hollow, "royalty is coming" sound:

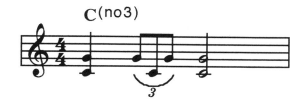

Other than a situation like the one above, the 5th is usually very expendable. To illustrate this point, consider the difference between these two examples:

<u>Example #1</u>

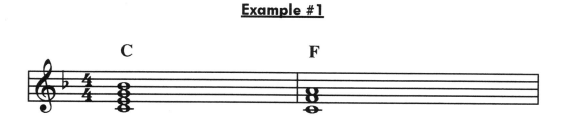

Example #2

Notice that when the 5th is left out (Example #2), the chord's integrity is not sacrificed. All the tendencies which exist when the chord contains the 5th, also exist when the 5th is left out. (Such is not the case with the 3rd or the b7th. The chord's "completeness" suffers noticeably when the 3rd or the b7th is left out.)

Because it's convenient, musicians usually include the 5th in triads and 7th chords. However, 9th, 11th and 13th chords are often voiced without the 5th. The 5th scale degree is a lot like a shy, unobtrusive friend who, even when he participates, is usually not very notable.

The #5th scale degree usually connotes pensiveness. When your favorite soap opera breaks for an advertisement, often the last thing you hear is a #5 chord. This is because you are watching the expression on Mary's face, as her wistful thoughts about Henry, Alice, Ted, Fred and Suzannah are mulled over:

The #5th is sometimes used for "falling-type" situations. This could be due to the fact that when people are actually in the act of falling, they can be quite pensive:

The #5th is also commonly used in "uplifting-type" situations:

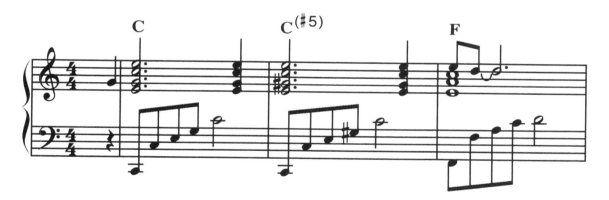

The 13th (or 6th) scale degree is sugary sweet:

This sugary sweet sound is due, in part, to the extremely low level of dissonance this scale degree creates. (Notice that the 13th is the more dissonant of the two, due to the inclusion of the b7th.) The 13th (or 6th) scale degree is very much like a friend who is so kind, considerate and all-accommodating, that you are almost uncomfortable around him.

The b7th scale degree is a very strong chord member. Like the 3rd, it helps preserve the rich harmonic color of virtually any chord. However, unlike the 3rd, its inclusion in a chord usually creates strong resolving tendencies:

As is the case in the example above, generally, the b7th scale degree wants to resolve to the 3rd scale degree of the next chord (as indicated by the arrows). The strong resolving tendencies created by the b7th scale degree make the dominant (V7) chord "dominate". However, one fairly uncommon exception to the b7th's desire to resolve is found in the I7 ending:

Because it is a very strong chord member, and it usually likes to resolve to the 3rd scale degree of the next chord, we can think of the b7th scale degree as a highly motivated harmonic bodyguard.

The 7th scale degree is also a very strong chord member. Like the 3rd and the b7th, it adds rich harmonic color to virtually any chord. It also can be thought of as a harmonic bodyguard.

The #7th scale degree usually creates an air of mystery. For this reason, it is used to suggest or depict slightly sinister or secret situations:

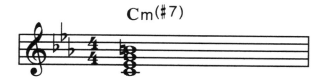

This scale degree is commonly used as part of a descending line:

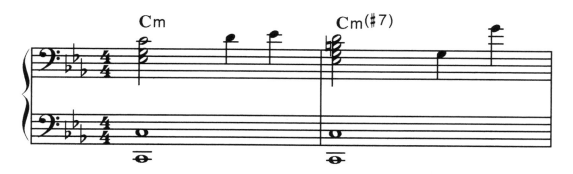

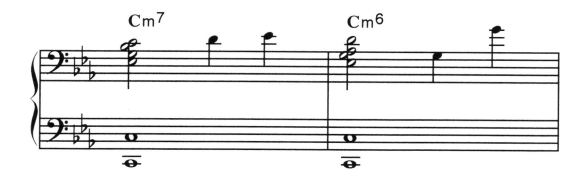

This scale degree is also commonly used as part of a circular melody:

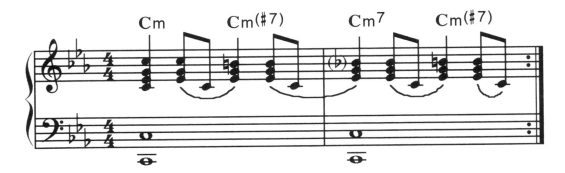

Understanding the personality and tendencies of each scale degree will assist you in your quest to learn how to add altered tones to your music:

Root	– central pitch
b9th	– temperamental
9th	– adaptable
#9th	– "good-time Charlie"
b3rd	– sad, gloomy
3rd	– harmonic bodyguard
11th or sus4	– temperamental
#11th or b5th	– yearning
5th	– shy, unobtrusive
#5th	– pensive
13th or 6th	– all-accommodating, sugary sweet
b7th	– highly motivated harmonic bodyguard
7th	– harmonic bodyguard
#7th	– mysterious, secretive

During the formation of melody, harmony and rhythm, scale degree personalities are combined. This combining results in the emergence of new personalities, in the same way that third personalities result from two or more people joining together.

NON-HARMONIC TONES AND RESOLVING DEVICES

Any note that is foreign to a particular chord symbol is referred to as a "non-harmonic tone" or a "non-chord tone". Non-harmonic tones have a knack for creating dissonance. The additional dissonance brought about by the inclusion of non-harmonic tones will add color to your harmony. However, this additional dissonance often adds both color and unrelieved tension...and unrelieved tension requires resolution.

Musicians use six devices to resolve unrelieved tension. These devices are named for the six types of non-harmonic tones that require resolution:

> Passing Tone
> Neighbor Tone
> Escape Tone
> Appoggiatura
> Anticipation
> Suspension

Before I cover the working definitions and examples of each, allow me to clarify some terminology:

strong beat: any accented beat. In rock music, beats 2 and 4 are the strong beats. In polkas, beats 1 and 3 are the strong beats.

weak beat: any unaccented beat. In rock music, beats 1 and 3 are the weak beats. In polkas, beats 2 and 4 are the weak beats.

These two term's meanings have been stretched to include portions of beats. For example:

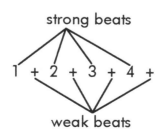

syncopation: accenting beats (or portions) which are normally unaccented. Syncopation at the eighth note level involves accenting the "+". Syncopation at the sixteenth note level involves accenting the "e" and/or the "a".

The following example illustrates eighth note level syncopation:

Notice that when syncopation occurs, the organization of strong and weak beats is reversed:

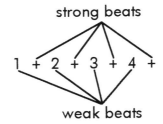

<u>step progression</u>:   notes proceeding by half steps and/or whole steps and/or augmented 2nds. (The term "chromatic" refers to progression by half steps, while the term "diatonic" means "occurring within the major (or minor) scale".

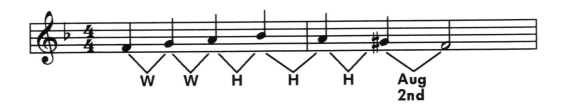

<u>leap progression</u>:   notes proceeding by intervals of a minor 3rd or larger.

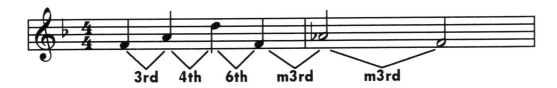

Here ends your terminology lesson. Now let's examine each resolving device.

A <u>passing tone</u> occurs on a weak beat, between two different chord members, amongst step progression. In the following example, the 11th is functioning as a passing tone.

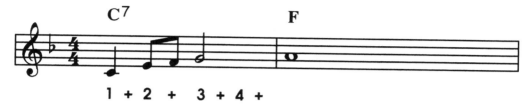

The note F is said to be a passing tone because it is struck while passing from chord member E to chord member G.

In this next example, the #11th is functioning as a passing tone:

Here's the b9th functioning as a passing tone:

The 9th as a passing tone:

The #9th as a passing tone:

The b5th as a passing tone:

The #5th as a passing tone:

The 13th as a passing tone:

The 6th as a passing tone:

The b7th as a passing tone:

The #7th as a passing tone:

A <u>neighbor tone</u> occurs between the same chord member, amongst step progression. In the following example, the 11th is functioning as a neighbor tone.

The note F is said to be a neighbor tone to the chord member E. The other notes that are able to function as neighbor tones to the chord member E are: F#, D#, D and Db.

Here's the #11th functioning as a neighbor tone:

The b9th as a neighbor tone:

The 9th as a neighbor tone:

The #9th as a neighbor tone:

The b5th as a neighbor tone:

The #5th as a neighbor tone:

The 13th as a neighbor tone:

The 6th as a neighbor tone:

The b7th as a neighbor tone:

The #7th as a neighbor tone:

An <u>escape tone</u> occurs on a weak beat, between either the same chord member or two different chord members, and involves at least one leap.

Here's the b9th functioning as an escape tone:

The 9th as an escape tone:

The #9th as an escape tone:

The 11th as an escape tone:

The #11th as an escape tone:

The b5th as an escape tone:

The #5th as an escape tone:

The 13th as an escape tone:

The 6th as an escape tone:

The b7th as an escape tone:

The #7th as an escape tone:

An <u>appoggiatura</u> occurs on a strong beat, and its resolution involves step progression.

Here's the b9th functioning as an appoggiatura:

The 9th as an appoggiatura:

The #9th as an appoggiatura:

The 11th as an appoggiatura:

The #11th as an appoggiatura:

The b5th as an appoggiatura:

The #5th as an appoggiatura:

The 13th as an appoggiatura:

The 6th as an appoggiatura:

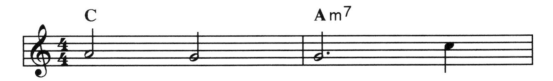

The b7th as an appoggiatura:

The #7th as an appoggiatura:

An <u>anticipation</u> occurs when a note from the next chord precedes that chord:

Here's the b9th functioning as an anticipation:

The 9th as an anticipation:

The #9th as an anticipation:

The 11th as an anticipation:

The #11th as an anticipation:

The b5th as an anticipation:

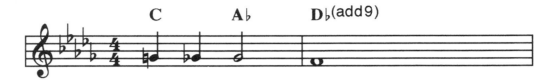

The #5th as an anticipation:

The 13th as an anticipation:

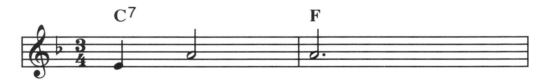

The 6th as an anticipation:

The b7th as an anticipation:

The #7th as an anticipation:

A <u>suspension</u> occurs when a note from the preceding chord is either held down or tied over.

Here's the b9th functioning as a suspension:

The 9th as a suspension:

The #9th as a suspension:

The 11th as a suspension:

The #11th as a suspension:

The b5th as a suspension:

The #5th as a suspension:

The 13th as a suspension:

The 6th as a suspension:

The b7th as a suspension:

The #7th as a suspension:

Four of the non-harmonic tones are commonly doubled. For example, here is a double appoggiatura:

Because two notes imply a chord, the ear may hear the double appoggiatura as a chord:

For the same reason, the ear may hear double passing tones as a "passing chord":

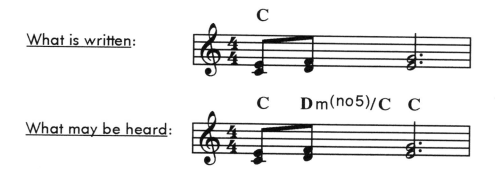

The ear may hear double neighbor tones as a "neighbor chord":

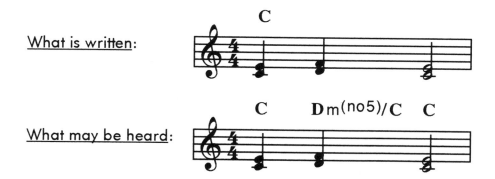

And the ear may hear double escape tones as an "escape chord":

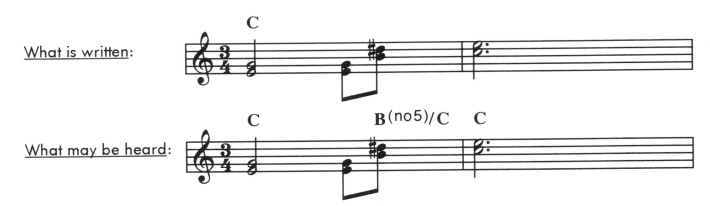

Any musician who becomes adept at non-harmonic tone resolution has no problems with "wrong" notes. When dissonance is created intentionally, through a musician's thought processes, it can be resolved through the use of one or more of the non-harmonic tone resolving devices. When dissonance is created unintentionally, through faulty thinking or a mistakenly placed finger, it also can be resolved through the use of one or more of the non-harmonic tone resolving devices. Eventually, you will get to the point where you're not sure whether a dissonance was created intentionally or unintentionally. Either way, it won't matter because, if a dissonance needs resolution, you'll know how to apply it. By this time, the keyboard will have become somewhat of a happy hunting ground — and every note is fair game.

<hr>

MODES

A mode is a collection of pitches from which is drawn the basic melodic and harmonic material of a composition. When this collection of pitches is arranged sequentially in ascending and/or descending order, the result is a scale.

Throughout this book, we have been dealing with the major mode and various minor modes. Now we will explore other modes used in the construction of music. They are:

Ionian
Dorian
Phrygian
Lydian
Mixolydian

Aeolian
Locrian
Pentatonic
Altered Pentatonic
Blues
Altered Blues
Whole Tone (or Augmented)
Diminished
Inverted Diminished
Altered Minor

A thorough understanding of these modes will be useful when analyzing or improvising melodies and harmonies.

The first seven modes can be formed using the notes of any major scale. Using the C scale as an example:

Ionian:	C	D	E	F	G	A	B	C
Dorian:	D	E	F	G	A	B	C	D
Phrygian:	E	F	G	A	B	C	D	E
Lydian:	F	G	A	B	C	D	E	F
Mixolydian:	G	A	B	C	D	E	F	G
Aeolian:	A	B	C	D	E	F	G	A
Locrian:	B	C	D	E	F	G	A	B

Notice that ionian is just another name for the major mode, and aeolian is just another name for the natural minor mode.

Mixolydian is used quite often, especially in popular music:

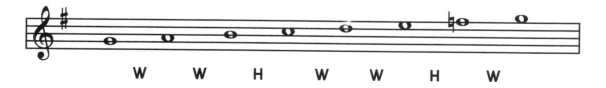

W   W   H   W   W   H   W

The only difference between G major and G mixolydian is a lowered 7th scale degree. This lowered 7th scale degree causes the F#dim chord to become a F major chord. So, what was the vii° chord in the major mode becomes a bVII chord in the mixolydian mode:

Like all other modes, mixolydian can begin on any note of the piano keyboard. C mixolydian looks like this:

F mixolydian looks like this:

and so on...

Dorian is also a commonly used mode:

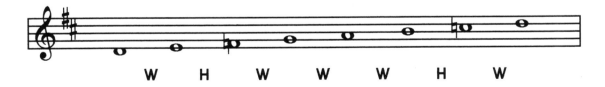

The only difference between major and dorian is a lowered 3rd and a lowered 7th. The lowered lowered 3rd places this mode closer to minor, than to major. Consequently, dorian is usually written using a minor key signature:

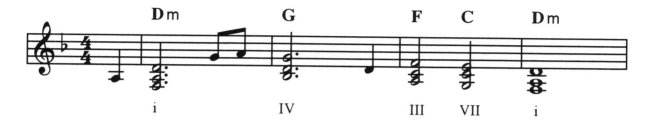

Lydian is the jazz mode:

The only difference between major and lydian is a raised 11th. This raised 11th is a primary characteristic of the jazz idiom. Be it understood as a #11th or a b5th, jazz musicians and jazz listeners love to be around this altered scale degree:

Phrygian is rarely found outside the jazz idiom. The difference between major and phrygian is a lowered 9th, 3rd, 6th and 7th:

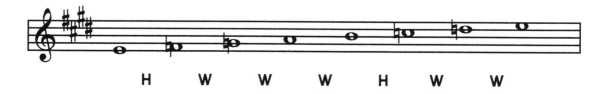

Phrygian contains four altered tones: b9th, b3rd (or #9th), #5th and b7th. Collectively, these altered tones give phrygian a spicey sound:

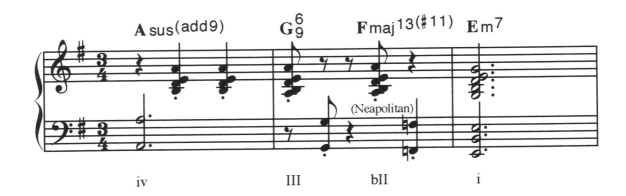

Locrian, also, is rarely found outside the jazz idiom. (In fact, it's rarely found anywhere.) The difference between major and locrian is a lowered 9th, 3rd, 5th, 6th and 7th:

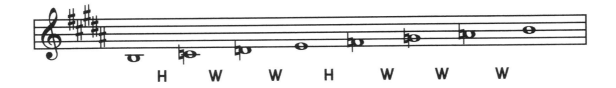

The tonic triad of locrian is a diminished chord. (In B locrian, the tonic triad is B, D, F.) While diminished chords may function many beautiful ways, they make lousy pitch centers. This is because music returns to its pitch center (i.e. tonic) for a sense of finality, yet diminished chords provide no such sense of finality. Instead, diminished chords provide an ambiguous sound, full of tension. Any time you are dealing with the locrian mode, you are bringing "instant weird" to your music:

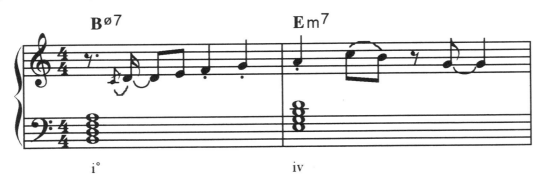

Locrian contains five altered tones: b9th, b3rd (or #9th), b5th (or #11th), #5th and b7th.

The pentatonic mode contains five notes:

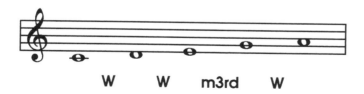

The difference between major and pentatonic is the absence of the 4th (or 11th) and 7th scale degrees. Here's pentatonic built on Gb:

Gb pentatonic makes the pentatonic mode extremely accessible: just stay on the black notes! Notice that when you play only black notes, no severe dissonance results, regardless of how many black notes you strike simultaneously. Here's why:

Remembering the earlier discussion about scale degree personalities, take a look at the components of the pentatonic scale:

> Root
> 9th
> 3rd
> 5th
> 6th

The only non-triad tones are the 9th and the 6th. Now, let's review what was said about the 9th and the 6th:

"The 9th scale degree is very adaptable. It fits in almost anywhere, almost anytime. Generally, the 9th will add a plush quality to your major chords."

"The 6th scale degree is sugary sweet. This sugary sweet sound is due, in part, to the extremely low level of dissonance this scale degree creates."

It is no small wonder that use of the pentatonic scale to form melodies and harmonies results in no severe dissonance. With the exclusion of the 4th and 7th scale degrees, no severe dissonance can result.

The pentatonic mode is often used to create an oriental sound, like:

or:

An altered pentatonic mode may be used when higher levels of dissonance are desired. Altered pentatonic scales may contain one or more of the following: b9th, #9th (or b3rd), b5th, #5th.

The blues mode is used, obviously enough, for the creation of blues music. The "blues" sound results from the use of this mode:

Two commonly used altered blues modes are:

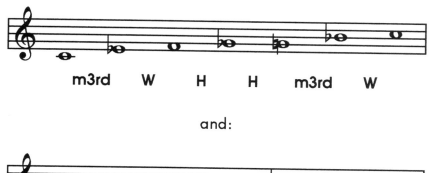

and:

The blues mode in action:

The whole tone (or augmented) mode is comprised of whole steps:

Use of this mode will usually produce a "lighter than air" type of sound:

The diminished mode is made up of alternating whole and half steps:

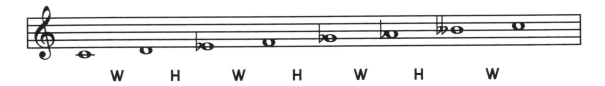

W   H   W   H   W   H   W

For ease of reading, this mode is usually written this way:

W   H   W   H   W   H   W

Use of this mode will instantly place you in ancient Persia: (...where you've always wanted to be)

The inverted diminished mode is made up of alternating whole and half steps. However, unlike its predecessor, this mode begins with a half step:

H   W   H   W   H   W   H

For ease of reading, this mode is usually written this way:

H   W   H   W   H   W   H

Like its predecessor, this mode is distinctly Persian:

Altered minor modes belong to the jazz idiom. Here is an example of an altered minor mode:

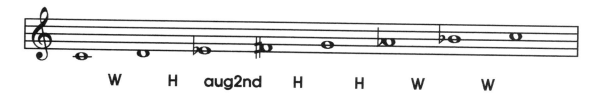

W   H   aug2nd   H   H   W   W

Notice that the alteration is jazz music's beloved #11th. The following example depicts what an altered minor mode might be caught doing on a Sunday afternoon:

DO I REALLY NEED TO KNOW THIS STUFF?

All of these modes are commonly used by jazz improvisation artists. However, for those of you who don't enjoy flirting with the jazz sound, it will help you to know which modes are in common use, considering all types of music prevalent in our culture.

Very Commonly Used Modes
> Ionian (or Major)
> Harmonic Minor
> Melodic Minor
> Mixolydian
> Dorian

Commonly Used Modes
> Lydian
> Pentatonic
> Blues
> Altered Blues
> Whole Tone (or Augmented)
> Altered Minor

Rarely Used Modes
> Phrygian
> Aeolian (or Natural Minor)
> Locrian
> Altered Pentatonic
> Diminished
> Inverted Diminished

CHAPTER NINE
ADVANCED PERFORMANCE

Dadgum! Did you ever think you'd make it this far? Hasn't it been fun? Haven't the long hours of intense concentration just "flown by"? Wasn't it great? Welcome to advanced performance!

At the advanced level, "dynamic" will become your middle name. While improving your "as written" abilities, you will learn exciting new ways to perform using chord symbols, and your ear training will evolve into the ultimate aural activity: improvisation!

"AS WRITTEN" APPROACH

Let's begin with the selection of your advanced "as written" music. There is an inexhaustible supply of music, both classical and popular, written and/or arranged for the advanced "as written" musician. I recommend focusing your attention on the music you enjoy the most. By now, you probably have several favorite composers. Concentrate your efforts on the music of these composers. However, I also recommend broadening your horizons by keeping at least one piece of music written by a "new" composer (i.e. you haven't played any of his music before) in your practice schedule. In doing this, you will open up many new avenues of "as written" study. Some of these "new" composers will join the ranks of your favorite composers.

As you enjoy developing your advanced "as written" abilities, keep this in mind: The process of learning challenging "as written" music never changes — unless you're able to sight-read the music at hand, the basic practice techniques will always apply.

ADAPTATION

At the advanced level, a new performance option will become available: the adaptation. The term "adaptation" refers to the performance of a song using a combination of the "as written" approach and any "chord symbol" approach. Quite obviously, adaptations can only result from two types of written music:

Two staves with chord symbols:

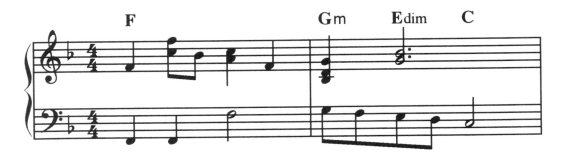

And three staves with chord symbols:

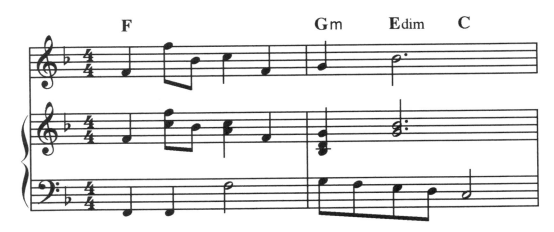

It is left up to you, the performer, to decide which portions of a song are arranged very nicely and consequently, will be performed "as written", and which portions of a song are thinly arranged and consequently, will be improved upon through the use of a "chord symbol" approach.

During an adaptation, you may also find yourself embellishing some "as written" portions. For instance, you may fill in missing chord members when a more full sound is desirable. Or you may change some rhythms so that your rendition more closely approximates the original version of a song. Occasionally, you will even change written melody notes or include missing melody notes.

In an adaptation, you are combining the best of two performance concepts:

1.) the original <u>arranger's</u> <u>ideas</u> on how a specific piece of music should be performed.

2.) <u>your</u> original <u>ideas</u> on how a specific piece of music should be performed.

(When you wish to adapt music which contains no chord symbols, you may choose to write in the chord symbols. This is easy to do. Simply determine which chord is being used, based on the notes that are written. Then, using a pencil, write the chord symbol which corresponds with the written notes.)

<u>"CHORD SYMBOL" APPROACH</u>

At the intermediate level, you learned the first three ways to perform using chord symbols: Two Hand Method, Three Hand Method and Arpeggiation Method. At the advanced level, you will learn the other three ways to perform using chord symbols: Chord Scale Improvisation, Non-Harmonic Tone Improvisation and Jazz/Modal Improvisation.

As a way to both cap off your intermediate chord symbol performance and introduce yourself to advanced chord symbol performance, I recommend learning the following diatonic 7th chord exercise:

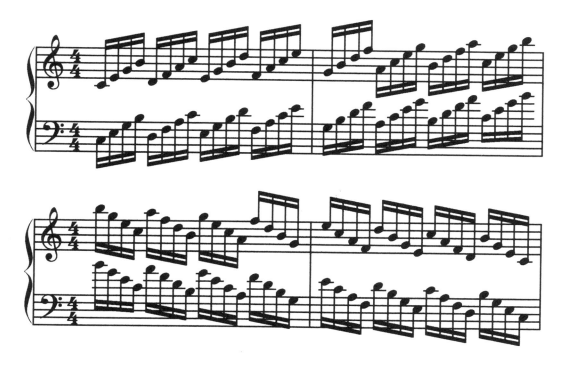

Note: transpose this exercise to all twelve major keys using the following pattern:

maj7	m7	m7	maj7	dom7	m7	⌀7	maj7
I	ii	iii	IV	V	vi	vii°	I

CHORD SCALE IMPROVISATION

Chord Scale Improvisation is, quite simply, Three Hand method, with the addition of 9ths and/or llths and/or 13ths in both the melody and the harmony. On the occasion of a repeat, or during vocal accompaniment, the written melody may be replaced with an improvised melody using the thematic development techniques found in chapter ten.

Begin your Chord Scale Improvisation by finding a song which fulfills two criteria:

> 1.) You enjoy listening to the song.

> 2.) You are already able to perform the song
> using Three Hand Method.

When you have located this piece of music, begin practicing it the following ways:

1.) While performing the song using Three Hand Method, practicing adding the 9th to each chord. This may be accomplished three ways:

1a.) Add the 9th to the solid (full or partial) chord:

<u>What is written</u>:

<u>What your right hand might play</u>:

1b.) Add the 9th between two melody notes. When necessary, use any of the six resolving devices:

<u>What is written</u>:

<u>What your right hand might play</u>:

1c.) If and when the 9th (or ♭9th or #9th) is written as a part of the melody or the harmony, circle it, label it, and recognize it as the 9th when you play through that chord or that chord's domain:

Though the song will become "nauseatingly ninthy", keep the faith and follow my directions.

Notice that 9ths may be added both vertically (as a part of solid chords) and horizontally (as melodic "fill" notes). You should not be including only vertical 9ths, or only horizontal 9ths. Rather, you should include a combination of the two:

When you are able to comfortably include 9ths throughout the song, move on to the next step.

2.) While performing the song using Three Hand Method, practice adding the 11th (or 4th) to each chord. (Add only the 11th, <u>not</u> the 9th and the 11th.) This is done the same way as when you added the 9th. However, you will notice one big difference: the 11th, being less adaptable than the 9th, will not fit as well in solid chords. Consequently, horizontal 11ths will be the rule; vertical 11ths will be the exception.

<u>What is written</u>:

<u>What your right hand might play</u>:

When you are able to comfortably include 11ths (and/or 4ths) throughout the song, move on to the next step.

3.) While performing the song using Three Hand Method, practice adding the 13th (or 6th) to each chord. (Add only the 13th, <u>not</u> the 9th, 11th and 13th.) This is done the same way that you added the 9th and the 11th. You will notice that the 13th is more adaptable than the 11th, and not quite as adaptable as the 9th. Again, you should be including a combination of vertical 13ths and horizontal 13ths.

<u>What is written</u>:

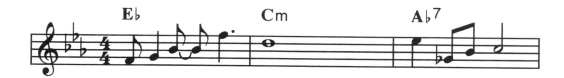

<u>What your right hand might play</u>:

When you are able to comfortably include 13ths (and/or 6ths) throughout the song, move on to the next step.

4.) Begin including 9ths, 11ths and 13ths in the left hand too:

<u>What is written</u>:

<u>What you might play:</u>

When you are able to include an occasional 9th, 11th or 13th in the left hand, move on to the last step. 5.) Don't think, just play. In regards to this first "Chord Scale" song, you have "programmed your computer". Your various forms of memory (muscular, aural, pattern) will have you automatically including as many 9ths, 11ths and 13ths as your ear finds desirable.

With enough practice on these five steps, you will develop the ability to transform an ordinary piece of music into a magnificent arrangement! Your foes will be amazed. (So will your friends.)

As was the case with Three Hand Method, eventually these five steps will become unnecessary. You will be able to spontaneously "Chord Scale" any music you wish, whether performing by adaptation, by chord symbol, or by ear.

For further study on Chord Scale Improvisation, refer to the thematic development techniques found in chapter ten.

PRE–HEARING

Now that you're a little baby "Chord Scaler", you've probably noticed a phenomenon taking place in your mind's ear: pre-hearing. For those of you who are mechanically adding the 9ths, 11ths and 13ths, and hence, may not have experienced pre-hearing, I will define it. Pre-hearing is listening to a note (or notes) in your mind's ear, prior to the actual performance of such note (or notes).

Pre-hearing may take place in the instant just prior to the note's performance (called "instant pre-hearing"), or it may occur several days or hours before an actual performance (called "latent pre-hearing").

An example of the former would be something like this: pre-hearing a 9th fitting into a chord in the instant just prior to the actual inclusion of the 9th in the performance of that chord. An example of the latter would be something like this: hearing an actual performance of a piece of music, and then retaining, in your mind's ear, the sound's you heard, so that when you are able to get to a piano, whether several days or several hours later, you will be capable of reproducing what was heard.

Instant pre-hearing, quite obviously, takes place during the actual performance of a piece of music and, as such, is an essential part of the thought processes necessary for meaningful improvisation. Latent pre-hearing relies heavily on a performer's ability to simultaneously detect and remember the songform, the chord progression (in terms of figured bass), the melody notes, and the rhythms used throughout a piece of music. The development of both instant and latent pre-hearing results in the process referred to as "playing by ear".

If you observe instant pre-hearing already taking place during your Chord Scale Improvisation, fine. If you don't observe instant pre-hearing taking place, don't worry. The process of mechanically adding the 9ths, 11ths and 13ths will eventually result in your becoming capable of pre-hearing 9ths, 11ths and 13ths.

It is extremely important to develop the ability to pre-hear, if for no other reason, because it removes doubt. You, the performer, having already pre-heard what you are about to play, are able to remain confident, and hence, comfortable. This confidence and solace are relayed to your listeners...including yourself.

NON–HARMONIC TONE IMPROVISATION

Non-Harmonic Tone Improvisation is the use of resolving devices so that not only 9ths, 11ths and 13ths may be easily included in your music, but also any of the altered tones. On the occasion of a repeat, or during vocal accompaniment, the written melody may be replaced with an improvised melody, using the thematic development techniques found in chapter ten. This is not to say that the only way to include 9ths, 11ths, 13ths and altered tones in your music is through the use of resolving devices. Depending on the context in which they are used, sometimes these extra notes need no resolution. However, it is more often the case that these extra notes do need resolving.

If these extra notes usually require a resolution, why do we, as performers, seek them out? Why do we want to create seemingly needless hassles? Well...it's because these extra notes add so much beauty to our music. These extra notes are aural delights! (It's easy to imagine how dull music would be if we just stayed on basic chord members all the time.)

To begin understanding Non-Harmonic Tone Improvisation, we should know some fundamental truths:

1.) There is <u>no</u> such thing as a wrong note.
2.) There <u>is</u> such a thing as a wrong resolution.

When a teacher says you struck a "wrong" note, he means the note you struck was not written in the music and/or the note you struck was very dissonant and left unresolved. Likewise, when a teacher says you struck several "wrong" notes simultaneously (i.e. a "wrong" chord), he means the notes you struck were not written in the *music and/or the notes you struck were very dissonant and left unresolved. However* whether you are playing music by note, by chord symbol, or by ear, when you strike a note or chord that sounds suspect (i.e. too dissonant), based on your study of the information in this book, you will be capable of resolving your way out of the melodic or harmonic trouble you got yourself into. Whether the dissonance was created deliberately or unintentionally doesn't matter. What <u>does</u> matter is this: When a dissonance requiring resolution occurs, a correct resolution should follow soon thereafter.

What is a correct resolution? Nothing more than the use of an appropriately fitting resolving device. Total familiarity with the six resolving devices (via practice) is all that is necessary for you to be able to instantly choose which device, or devices, will get you out of trouble most effectively. Having defined correct resolution, allow me to define the opposite: wrong resolution. A wrong resolution is any of the following, occurring immediately after a dissonance which requires resolution:

1.) Playing on, as if no strong dissonance, requiring resolution, ever occurred.

2.) Stopping (i.e. pausing or hesitating).

3.) Saying: "Oops, I hit a wrong note."

4.) Cursing.

5.) Flinching.

6.) Any other habitually nervous reaction, such as whistling, twitching, shaking your head, etc.

By learning to use correct resolutions, dissonance and "wrong" notes will cease to be your enemies. Instead, they will become your partners in crime...you'll be able to get away with all kinds of neat sounding things.

By the way, just because a note (or notes) is labelled "wrong" doesn't mean it will sound ugly. Quite often, "wrong" notes are not strongly dissonant. As such, of course, these "wrong" notes may require no resolution. Whether they require resolution or not, all "wrong" notes are inadvertent, yet colorful, additions to a melody or a harmony. And, though it may seem paradoxical, dissonance, when handled correctly, is a very important ingredient in quality music.

The process of learning Non-Harmonic Tone Improvisation is different for everybody. Some people will begin to pre-hear altered tones along with the 9ths, 11ths and 13ths used in Chord Scale Improvisation. For these lucky people, Non-Harmonic Tone Improvisation will occur naturally, as a direct result of their Chord Scaling experience. However, most people will begin to add altered tones only after carefully studying them. For these people, the process of pre-hearing extra notes does not readily take place. Until pre-hearing abilities are strengthened, a methodological approach is necessary. Here are some suggestions:

1.) Study the examples found in chapter eight. Play them and listen!

2.) Look through written music until you find an altered tone. Observe the melodic, harmonic and rhythmic conditions which allow the altered tone to "fit in". Also, notice which, if any, resolving devices are used. Play through the phrase of music which contains the altered tone. Listen to the altered tone "fitting in". Look through more written music until you find another altered tone and repeat the process, etc.

3.) Look for situations where the inclusion of an altered tone will not violate the key signature.

For example: When an F chord occurs as the IV chord in the key of C, the note B (the #11th) will generally fit in as well, or better, than the note Bb (the 11th). Listen to the following examples:

<u>What is written</u>:

<u>What you might play</u>:

<u>Or you might play this</u>:

Notice the note B (the #11th) fits like a glove. When beginning Non-Harmonic Tone Improvisation, some people will find altered tones which comply with the key signature easier to pre-hear than altered tones which violate the key signature.

Here is another example: When an Em chord occurs as a iii chord in the key of C, the note F (the b9th) will generally fit in as well, or better, than the note F# (the 9th). Listen:

<u>What is written</u>:

<u>What you might play</u>:

<u>Or you might play this</u>:

[Note: It should be understood that an altered tone should not be played simultaneously with the original (un-altered) tone. In other words, a #5th should not be played simultaneously with the 5th; a b9th should not be played simultaneously with the 9th, etc. Either the altered tone is used, or the original (un-altered) tone is used — but not both at the same time, in the same chord. Horizontally? Yes, it's okay to use the #5th with the 5th, or the b9th with the 9th. Vertically? Absolutely not, unless you're writing the score to a horror movie, or you just feel like creating repugnant sounds.]

When you feel like your brain is programmed, choose a song you wish to use to initiate Non-Harmonic Tone Improvisation. Play the song using Three Hand Method. Then play it using Chord Scale Improvisation. Then seek out opportunities to include altered tones. Experiment! Use some vertical (harmonic) altered tones and some horizontal (melodic) altered tones. If, in an entire song, you only find one or two places to include an altered tone, don't get green-faced with yourself. Instead, repeat the process on another song...and another, etc. You will find that some songs seem to accept altered tones more willingly than others. Fine. No sweat. Don't force the issue with the "unwilling" songs. Instead, milk the "willing" songs. (Just keep in mind it's your ear that is responsible for your successes and failures, not the songs themselves.)

Eventually, having gone through all these cognitive processes, you should begin the "don't think, just play" process. Your various forms of memory (muscular, aural, pattern) will have you automatically including an occasional altered tone, along with the occasional 9ths, 11ths and 13ths.

You may use NHT Improvisation when performing by adaptation, by chord symbol, or by ear.

For further study on NHT Improvisation, refer to the thematic development techniques found in chapter ten.

SUMMARY OF THE "CHORD SYMBOL" APPROACH

Back when you were learning Two Hand Method, Three Hand Method and Arpeggiation Method, you were taught the chord symbol "C meant that you were to use the notes C, E and G for your harmony. Any note, other than these three chord members, was considered wrong. So, the notes Db, D, Eb, F, Gb, Ab, Bb and B were "off limits".

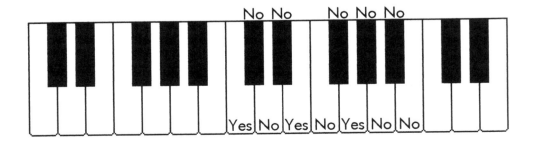

When you began Chord Scale Improvisation, you were taught the chord symbol "C" meant that you may use the notes C, E, G, B, D, F and A for your harmony and your melody. Any note, other than these seven chord members, was considered wrong. So, the notes Db, Eb, Gb, Ab and Bb were "off limits". (Note: When a C chord functions as a dominant 7th, quite obviously, Bb replaces B.)

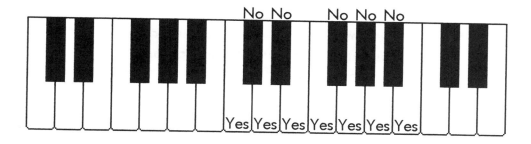

Then you began Non-Harmonic Tone Improvisation and were taught the chord symbol "C" meant that you could use any notes for your harmony and your melody. You discovered that there are no wrong notes, just wrong resolutions. "Off limit" notes don't exist; "off limit" resolutions do.

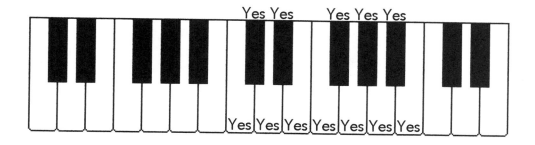

Obviously, these concepts are transferable to any major chord and, provided the necessary scale degree adjustments are made, these concepts are transferable to any minor, diminished, augmented, special instruction chord, etc.

By the time you are a capable "Chord Scaler" and "NHTer", a chord symbol represents this message from the composer:

"I recommend you, the performer, center
your improvisational activities around
the notes contained in this chord symbol."

Consequently, to the improvisation artist, a chord symbol represents little more than a point of departure.

CHAPTER TEN
ADVANCED EAR

Chapter four covers the basics of ear training. Chapter seven is concerned with the actual process of playing by ear. This chapter is devoted to the next logical step: spontaneous aural development of melody, harmony and rhythm. You have already done a lot of this. Arpeggiation Method, Chord Scale Improvisation and Non-Harmonic Tone Improvisation — each is spontaneous aural development of music. So, coming into this chapter, you've got a big head start. Let's take another view of this phenomenon through the study of Jazz Improvisation and Modal Improvisation.

JAZZ IMPROVISATION AND MODAL IMPROVISATION

All music, as we know it, is modal — that is, it is constructed using a collection of pitches (called a "mode") as a base from which to operate when forming melodies and harmonies. Musicians use the label "Modal Improvisation" to refer to improvisation which makes use of more than just the major and minor modes.

Not all jazz music is Modal Improvisation. However, virtually all Modal Improvisation falls under the heading of "jazz". Two notable exceptions are Gregorian chant and rock music's use of mixolydian or dorian improvisations.

Let's approach Jazz Improvisation and Modal Improvisation from two angles: transcription, and thematic development.

TRANSCRIPTION

The term "transcribe" refers to the process of writing out your "by ear" arrangements on music paper. You may ask: "Hey, if I can play a piece of music by ear, why should I bother to write it down?" Your answer: The transcription process presents an excellent learning situation. Also, having your arrangements in "as written" form or "chord symbol" (i.e. lead sheet) form makes for easy analysis, sharing and storage.

You have already done some basic transcription when you wrote out note heads and chord symbols during your study of chapter seven. However, a complete transcription should include exact rhythmic notation of both melody and harmony. Rhythmic transcription will have a profound effect on your ability to read, understand and "feel" rhythm. Also, it permits easy rhythmic analysis and, when you share your transcriptions with fellow musicians, removes any rhythmic guesswork.

At first, rhythmic transcription is not easy. After hearing a rhythm, you must visualize what that rhythm will look like in print, then write it out and re-check it. Often, counting out loud, while listening to a rhythm, will make the visualization process easier. If you find that you are unable to notate rhythms by ear, the practice of taking rhythmic dictation will alleviate the problem.

Begin rhythmic dictation study by recording yourself on cassette, playing written rhythms, one or two phrases in length, using a single note. For example, if the written music looks like this:

you would record yourself playing this:

Identify each recorded segment, so that you may eventually return to the written rhythm in order to check your work. When you have successfully recorded approximately twenty segments, stop recording, rewind the cassette tape and begin taking rhythmic dictation.

Listen to the first segment. Immediately stop the tape and proceed to write down the rhythm you just heard. If you need to listen to the segment several times, do so. If you have trouble visualizing what the segment is supposed to look like in written form, then determine the rhythm level and the time signature, and write the counting underneath the staff. [Note: Time signatures fall into two categories: <u>duple</u>, which is the "feel" of two (or four) beats per measure, and <u>triple</u>, which is the "feel" of three (or six) beats per measure. Music which is written in $\frac{2}{4}$ can credibly be written in $\frac{4}{4}$. Likewise, music which is written in $\frac{6}{8}$ can credibly be written in a fast $\frac{3}{4}$. My point: When determining the time signature, listen for the "angular" feel of duple $>$ $>$ $>$ $>$ or the "round" feel of triple $>$ $>$ (1 + 2 + 3 + 4 +), (1 2 3 1 2 3), and then determine a time signature that will work. Don't split hairs.] Using the example given, your written counting will look like this:

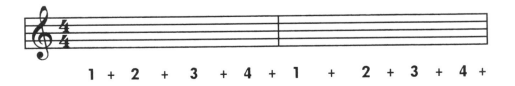

1 + 2 + 3 + 4 + 1 + 2 + 3 + 4 +

Count out loud while listening to the segment. Notice which symbols contain notes. This may take several listenings. Then begin writing single note heads above those symbols which contain notes. Using the example given, your music will look like this:

Then, using the written counting as a guide, write in the correct note values. Your finished product:

Check your work against the previously identified written rhythm. Then move on to the next recorded segment and repeat the process.

When you are able to notate a segment, after only one or two listenings, rhythmic dictation study, per se, will become unnecessary. You will have acquired the ability to transcribe rhythm.

Before transcribing Jazz/Modal Improvisation, please go back and transcribe the arrangements you made during your study of chapter seven. Depending on how quickly your aural abilities develop, you may also need to transcribe many more arrangements to obtain the ability to "jerk and write" Jazz/Modal Improvisation. The following two tidbits will ease some pain:

1.) At first, it is extremely important that you transcribe only songs which you enjoy hearing. Aural attraction gives the transcription process a big boost.

2.) "As written" transcription may take many hours per song, so, unless particular voicings are important to an arrangement, I recommend using the "chord symbol" (lead sheet) form for your transcriptions. This will save you time, energy and needless hassle.

The two problems inherent in Jazz/Modal Improvisation transcription are:

1.) Discerning individual notes from wickedly fast melodic passages.
2.) Notating jazz rhythm.

Problem #1 is easily overcome by listening to the music at half speed. Listen to a 33 1/3 RPM record at 16 RPM. The melodic passages you are attempting to discern will be slowed to half speed, will remain in the same key, and will be heard one octave lower. (Use of this technique is also possible with a two-speed reel-to-reel tape recorder or a two-speed cassette.)

Problem #2 is not easily conquered. Our system of rhythmic notation is incapable of representing the extremely subtle variations of duration which occur during the performance of jazz music. At times, your transcription of jazz rhythm will have to be an approximation.

Upon completion of each Jazz/Modal Improvisation transcription, you may opt to do some figured bass analysis. Also, you may look for the various ways arpeggiation, chord scales and non-harmonic tones are being used. Have fun!

Author's note: Please refer to Appendix Two for examples of my Jazz/Modal Improvisation transcriptions.

THEMATIC DEVELOPMENT

Development is the process of changing melody, harmony or rhythm. Thematic development is the process of changing melody — both structurally and rhythmically.

The devices a thematic developer might use are:

> Inversion
> Retrograde
> Retrograde Inversion

Truncation
Extension
Repetition
Sequencing
Cross Rhythm (or Hemiola)
Diminution
Augmentation
Counter Melody
Descant
Stretto
Composite Melody

Many great classical composers used these devices in the construction of their music. Likewise, many fine improvisation artists use these devices in the spontaneous construction of their music.

Before we begin examining each of these devices, we should have a motive to use as an example. We will label this motive "original" because it is the initial, unchanged melodic material which we are about to develop.

Original:

It is important that any original motive be uncomplicated. This allows for development.

Inversion

To invert a motive, simply turn each interval upside-down. For example, where your original motive goes up a 5th, your inverted motive will go down a 5th.

There are two types of inversion: real inversion and modified inversion. During real inversion, a musician will invert the intervals exactly as they occur in the original motive. During modified inversion, a musician will invert the intervals in such a way that the key signature is not violated. This means that a musician, in order to comply with a key signature, will change some minor intervals to major intervals and visa versa.

Real Inversion:

Modified Inversion:

<u>Our original motive</u>: up a 5th; down a 2nd; up a 3rd; down a 4th.
<u>The real inversion</u>: down a 5th; up a 2nd; down a 3rd; up a 4th.
<u>The modified inversion</u>: down a 5th; up a 2nd; down a minor 3rd; up a 4th.

Modified inversions are commonplace, while real inversions occur rarely. (Hereafter, when I use the term "inversion", it will mean "modified inversion".)

Retrograde

The retrograde of our original motive is simply the notes played in reverse order.

Retrograde:

Retrograde Inversion

As the name implies, retrograde inversion is both backwards and upside-down. (When you learn to think this way, you will be a true musician.)

Retrograde Inversion:

Truncation

The term "truncate" refers to the process of leaving out a portion of the motive. A musician may truncate the beginning, middle or end of a motive.

Extension

The term "extend" refers to the process of adding new melodic material. A musician may extend the beginning, middle or end of a motive.

Repetition

The term "repetition" obviously refers to the process of repeating. There are three basic types of repetition:

Melodic Repetition: (rhythm varies)

Rhythmic Repetition: (melody varies)

Melodic-Rhythmic Repetition: (no variation, just plain, good, old-fashioned repeating)

Sequencing

     The term "sequence" refers to the process of repeating a motive on a different pitch. Like the inversion process, sequences occur in "real" and "modified" form. In a real sequence, the intervals remain exactly the same as in the original motive. In a modified sequence, the intervals are changed in such a way that the key signature is not violated.

Real Sequence:

Modified Sequence:

Modified sequences are commonplace, while real sequences occur rarely. (Hereafter, when I use the term "sequence", it will mean "modified sequence".)

     With the possible exception of repetition, sequencing occurs more often than any other melodic development device. The reason for sequencing's popularity probably lies in the fact that it is an excellent way to combine some aspects of a "used" melodic idea with "new" melodic material. Sequencing represents a pleasant balance between, and combination of, something old and something new. However, like any thematic development device, sequencing, when used in excess, quickly becomes boring. Generally, three sequenced repetitions of the original melodic idea is plenty.

Cross Rhythm
(or Hemiola)

A cross rhythm occurs when a rhythm implies a different meter against the actual meter being played. Note that some of the following examples contain one or more of these thematic development devices: truncation, inversion, repetition, and extension.

$\frac{3}{8}$ being implied in $\frac{4}{4}$:

$\frac{2}{4}$ being implied in $\frac{3}{4}$:

$\frac{6}{8}$ being implied in $\frac{3}{4}$:

$\frac{3}{4}$ being implied in $\frac{6}{8}$:

The terms "hemiola" and "cross rhythm" are used interchangeably. Cross rhythm or hemiola — they dramatically heighten rhythmic interest.

Diminution

The term "diminution" refers to the process of making a musical element become gradually smaller. There are three types of diminution:

<u>Melodic Diminution</u> occurs when the number of notes in a motive gradually decreases:

<u>Rhythmic Diminution</u> occurs when the duration of notes is gradually shortened:

<u>Intervallic Diminution</u> occurs when interval size gradually decreases:

Various types of diminution may be combined:

Augmentation

The term "augmentation" refers to the process of making a musical element become gradually larger. There are three types of augmentation:

Melodic Augmentation occurs when the number of notes in a motive gradually increases:

Rhythmic Augmentation occurs when the duration of notes is gradually lengthened:

Intervallic Augmentation occurs when interval size gradually increases:

Various types of augmentation may be combined:

POLYPHONIC THEMATIC DEVELOPMENT DEVICES

The term "polyphonic" is used to describe music which contains two or more distinct melodies. Counter melody, descant, stretto and composite melody are thematic development devices commonly used to create polyphonic music.

Counter Melody

Counter melody is a general term used to describe any secondary melody which opposes (counters) the primary melody. Counter melody usually functions as melodic "filler" during gaps created by held tones or rests in the primary melody. However, a counter melody's notes may, on occasion, be struck simultaneously with the primary melody's notes.

In written music, a divided line is often used to separate the counter melody from the primary melody:

(Note: The term "counter melody" is sometimes written as one word — "countermelody".)

Descant

Any counter melody which occurs above the primary is called a "descant". Descants have a knack for creating aural fascination. When musicians sandwich the primary melody between a harmony and a descant, the resulting "wall of sound" mesmerizes many listeners.

Stretto

Stretto is the repetition of a motive, in a second voice-part, before the first voice-part has completed its statement of the motive. No secondary melody exists, as both voice-parts are considered to be of equal importance.

A "round" or a "canon" is simply stretto applied to an entire theme, instead of just a motive.

Composite Melody

When two distinct melodies of equal importance alternate phrases, the result is what musicians call a "composite melody". Composite melodies grab listeners ears by placing one melody "on hold", while the other melody gets its "licks" in. A composite melody occurring between two musicians is called a "dogfight".

Now that you understand the various devices used in thematic development, you should return to your transcriptions and locate these devices in the context of someone else's improvised line. One of the first things you will notice is that each device commonly occurs simultaneously with one or more other devices: sequencing while extending; inverting while truncating; even rhythmic diminution occurring during intervallic augmentation.

Along with your transcription study, go ahead and compose your own motives. Take each of your motives through all of the thematic development devices. Then practice your motives using two devices simultaneously. In the process of doing all of this, you will be programming your favorite computer — your musical mind.

When your improvised melody lines begin flowing comfortably and easily (later this decade), add left hand chord voicings. If and when a more full sound is desired, consider using both hands to voice your chords. I recommend learning various chord voicings and harmonic rhythm through imitation of your favorite styles. Obtain examples by referring to your own or someone else's transcriptions. [Note: You will quickly observe a general rule for voicing chords: spread the chord members (i.e. use larger intervals) to decrease dissonance and, conversely, condense the chord members (i.e. use smaller intervals) to increase dissonance.]

COMPOSER'S DISEASE AND COMPOSER'S DILEMMA

As a budding improvisation artist, you are a composer who writes his music spontaneously while performing it. As such, you should be aware of two maladies: "composer's disease" and "composer's dilemma".

Composer's disease is simple. It goes something like this:

"...yeah, but if I'd have written it, I'd have done it this way..."

There is no known cure.

Composer's dilemma is somewhat more complex. Every composer faces the same dilemma: unity versus variety. Any musical element or device which provides music with predictability is said to be a "unifying factor". For example, the thematic development device "repetition" functions primarily as a unifying factor. Conversely, any musical element or device which provides music with unpredictability is said to be a "variety factor". For example, the thematic development device "extension" functions primarily as a variety factor. When people become extremely predictable, we sometimes label them "nerds". Likewise, when music becomes extremely predictable, we might label it "uncool". (We might also vacate the premises.) When people become extremely unpredictable, we sometimes label them "prime candidates for the batty hatch". Likewise, when music becomes extremely unpredictable, we might wonder out loud about the "fried brains that scrambled that mess together". Too much unity is offensive. Too much variety is offensive. The composer's dilemma: maintain an acceptable balance between the two.

One object of the game of composition is: build up tension, then provide a release. To maintain an acceptable balance between unity and variety, you must become acutely aware of the "tension – release" phenomenon occurring in your music.

A unifying factor (or factors) may be used to build up tension:

A variety factor (or factors) may be used to build up tension:

A unifying factor (or factors) may be used to provide a release:

A variety factor (or factors) may be used to provide a release:

Note that variety is used to provide a release from tension brought about by unity. Conversely, unity is used to provide a release from tension brought about by variety. You, the composer, are constantly flirting with too much unity or too much variety; are continually tempering predictability with unpredictability, and unpredictability with predictability; are the sole arbitrator in the great musical challenge: unity versus variety.

Author's note: For further study of the jazz idiom, I highly recommend the Jamey Aebersold series of books, CD's, and play-a-long tapes. I also recommend any books by John Mehegan, Bill Dobbins or Mark Levine. Serious jazz students will find that all four of these authors offer outstanding teaching approaches.

CHAPTER ELEVEN
A SHORT BIOGRAPHY OF THE PIANO

The piano was born in 1709 in Florence, Italy. Its father, Bartolommeo Cristofori, named his invention "gravicembalo col piano e forte" — a "keyboard instrument that can be played soft and loud". I'm glad somebody shortened the name to "piano". I shudder to think of myself as a "gravecembaloist" or, worse yet, a "fortist". To this day, some people still refer to the instrument as a "piano-forte" — "soft-loud". However, most people feel more akin to the instrument and remain on a first name basis.

The English translation of "pianist" is "softist". However, most piano students start out as "fortists" ("loudists") and then quickly learn that the piano offers a wide range of dynamic possibilities. In my case, "quickly" was eight years. My parents claim their ears are still ringing.

Early pianos were crude and unsophisticated compared to modern-day instruments. In fact, it wasn't until the 1820's that the piano became like what we know it as today. It is one of the most popular and versatile instruments. With proper care and maintenance, a piano's life span is at least several hundred years.

CHAPTER TWELVE
AN OPEN LETTER TO PIANO TEACHERS AND PIANO STUDENTS

Music is ear. (Deaf people go to a musical performance primarily to watch.) The musician who has developed keenly perceptive listening abilities, along with note and chord symbol performance skills, is at a decided advantage. While "one way" musicians must slowly adapt to certain performing situations, the "three way" musican excels in any performing situation.

It is my observation that, on the whole, private piano instruction worldwide is void of all but the most primitive aural training. If music is ear, why aren't private piano instructors stressing aural learning at least as much as written (by note) learning? The answer to this question lies in the fact that piano teachers are also musicians. As musicians, piano instructors are extremely aware of their own limitations and are very careful not to exceed the limits of their skill level. Consequently, they feel like imposters if they teach something which they, themselves, are incapable of doing. These piano instructors are products of a learning environment created by their piano teachers, who also were deficient in their development of aural ability. Those who were taught only by note, in turn, teach only by note. A piece of paper with notes on it makes the abstract seem more tangible. However, the cost of dealing only with "paper music" is paid for with many unhappy, unfulfilled music students. Is it not our obligation, as piano instructors, to universalize, instead of specializing in only "as written" music, so that we may offer to our students a much more dynamic approach to the learning process?

For too long, we have thought of people who play by ear as "talented". If this were true, every student I have brought through the intermediate level is talented. While talent may play a big part in a person's teaching himself how to play by ear, this does not mean that all "ear" performers are talented, any more than all "as written" performers are talented. Playing by ear, like playing by note or by chord symbol, is an ability which can be taught. Indeed, playing by chord symbol and by ear should be taught. We, as music teachers, must be the first to remember that music is ear.

I am not saying that every student will want, or should want to learn all three ways to play the piano. I am saying that we, as teachers, should become competent at all three ways to play the piano, so that our students, in turn, are offered the "chord symbol" approach and the "by ear" approach, not just as "side dishes", but as an integral part of the main course. If we teachers choose not to universalize, we then choose to alienate many fine piano students, who gradually discover that the main course of study we offer them is incomplete, unpalatable and mainly coarse...(couldn't resist).

Many times we piano teachers get up on our tiny pedestals and exclaim: "My way! My terms or not at all!" My response to this attitude: Some of my most gratifying teaching experiences are the direct result of my meeting piano students on their terms and mine. My position is this: Working with the student, instead of working on or at the student, results in a very healthy learning atmosphere. I probably don't need to tell you that my ability to relate all three ways to play the piano plays a big part in this healthy "meeting of terms".

Many times I have heard piano teachers hide behind this excuse: "Well, if little Johnny learns to play by ear, he may never develop the self-discipline necessary to learn by note." While this statement is true, the dilemma it describes is easily overcome: Give note reading a head start. Teach little Johnny by note until his note reading skills are at an intermediate level. Then introduce the "chord symbol" approach. Finally, when note reading skills are at a high intermediate level, and the "chord symbol" approach is arriving at Three Hand Method, introduce playing by ear. (The "chord symbol" approach will bridge the gap between playing by note and playing by ear.) A lot of incentive is created when students realize there is more to music lessons than just processing dots on lines and spaces.

I have also heard piano teachers say this: "I'll teach you this way and then you can figure out the other on your own." The mysterious "other" is the "chord symbol" approach and the "ear" approach described in this book. If we, as music teachers, ignore the other two ways to play the piano, very few students will discover them on their own.

Some teachers may ask: "Will time spent learning by chord symbol or learning by ear detract from learning by note?" After more than two decades of teaching all three ways to play the piano. I can tell you the answer to this question: No. Obviously, if you want to get better at "as written" skills, you should practice "as written" music. However, not so obviously, if you want to get better at "as written" skills, you should practice "chord symbol" and "ear" music. Reasons? Sharpened aural memory and strengthened pattern memory, to name two. Result? Faster "as written" learning. I have demonstrated, time and again, through the accellerated learning which takes place in my students, that each way you learn to play the piano supports the others.

One side-benefit of teaching all three ways to play the piano: heightened interest, on the part of both the student <u>and</u> the teacher. If I were teaching only by note, my job would be considerably less fulfilling, and my students would be deprived of a full two-thirds of their musical satisfaction. Watching students blossom from "non-musician" to "partial keyboard musician" to "complete keyboard musician" is flat-out exciting. To be capable of bringing students only to the level of "partial keyboard musician", because I, myself, was a "partial keyboard musician", would be considerably less rewarding — both for me and for my students.

There are three ways to play the piano. Why not avail yourself, and eventually your students, to the new performance galaxies available to you through the practical application of the information contained in this book?

Finally, I want to say that music, like any other language, is meant to communicate. While many profound musical thoughts are communicated through "as written" recitation, a musician does not truly "speak" the language of music until he is able to make the transition from reproducing someone else's musical thoughts to actually using performance as an outlet for spontaneously created original musical thoughts. Command of a language is much more than the ability to recite well. Until we, as teachers, make available the learning systems which effectively allow a student to move from recitation to improvisation, those students who wish to do more than recite will be forced to join the ranks of the self taught. Does it really make sense — sending all these people out to "reinvent the wheel"? The learning systems exist. Let's use them!

APPENDIX 1
THE CLASSIFICATION OF INTERVALS

There are five types of intervals: perfect, major, minor, diminished and augmented. The unison (i.e. two tones of the same pitch sounding together; also called "prime"), 4th, 5th and 8th are <u>perfect</u> intervals. The 2nd, 3rd, 6th and 7th are <u>major</u> intervals. Major intervals lowered by one half step become <u>minor</u> intervals. Perfect intervals (with the exception of the unison) lowered by one half step, and major intervals lowered by one whole step become <u>diminished</u> intervals. Perfect intervals and major intervals raised by one half step become <u>augmented</u> intervals.

One half step higher is <u>augmented</u>.

Perfect
- U
- 4th
- 5th
- 8th

One half step lower is <u>diminished</u> (except the unison, because it is already the smallest possible interval).

Major
- 2nd
- 3rd
- 6th
- 7th

One half step lower is <u>minor</u>.

One whole step lower is <u>diminished</u>.

[Note: It is important to understand that an interval's numerical distance is measured alphabetically. For example, C to D# is an augmented 2nd (C to D is a spread of two notes: C D), while C to Eb is a minor 3rd (C to E is a spread of three notes: C D E); C to A is a major 6th (C to A is a spread of six notes: C D E F G A), while C to Bbb is a diminished 7th (C to B is a spread of seven notes: C D E F G A B).]

WHY ARE PERFECT INTERVALS CALLED "PERFECT"?

In researching the answer to this question, I found five separate sources with five varying reasons explaining why perfect intervals are called "perfect". Only one of the initial five sources turned out to be correct, demonstrating to me the amount of confusion which surrounds the term "perfect".

One source correctly states that a perfect interval, when inverted, will yield a perfect interval. For example, the 4th (C to F) inverts to a 5th (F to C); the unison (C and C) inverts to an 8th (C to C). However, another source incorrectly states that perfect intervals are called "perfect" <u>because</u> they invert to perfect intervals. This makes no more sense than saying that augmented triads are perfect chords because they invert to augmented triads, or full diminished seventh chords are perfect chords because they invert to full diminished seventh chords. Absolute hogwash!

Here is the correct explanation of why the term "perfect" is used in the classification of intervals: Pleasant-sounding intervals are referred to as "consonances". Unpleasant-sounding intervals are referred to as "dissonances". Consonances and dissonances have varied throughout time. Back in the Middle Ages, the Church attempted (with a high degree of success) to dictate which intervals would be consonant and which intervals would be dissonant. Consonant intervals were labeled "perfect", while dissonant intervals were labeled "imperfect". The intervals which would earn you a higher place in heaven were: the unison (or "prime"), 4th, 5th and 8th. Spiritually healthy listening meant avoiding the "imperfect" intervals. The Church didn't receive much flak about this idea, probably because long before their doctrine was handed down, the Greeks held that the consonant intervals were those whose arithmatical ratios were simple: the octave, 2:1, the 5th, 3:2, and the 4th, 4:3. (The Greeks decision seems to have been based as much on mathematics as on actual listening.)

Today, having slithered out from under the influence of the Church's musical doctrines, we consider the following intervals to be consonances: the unison, 3rd, 5th, 6th, 8th, minor 3rd and minor 6th. All other intervals are considered dissonances except the 4th which, depending on specific usage, may function either way. Yet, we still refer only to unisons, 4ths, 5ths and 8ths as "perfect".

Perfect: 1. Without defect; flawless. 2. Accurate; exact. Let's closely examine each of the "perfect" intervals from the standpoint of tuning to see just how "flawless" and "exact" they actually are. Our currently accepted method of tuning keyboard instruments is called "equal temperament". In this method of tuning, all 5ths are tempered (flatted) varying amounts so as to prevent all 3rds (the primary components of harmony) from being unbearably sharp. (For example, C to G is tempered so that Eb to G won't sound intolerably sharp.) Because 5ths invert to 4ths, you can't adjust one without having an effect on the other. There also exists a concept called "spread" which calls for octaves to be tuned increasingly sharp as you move towards the upper end of the keyboard. This results in a "bright" treble sound which many musicians find desirable. Unisons are tuned perfectly, but because there is no distance between two tones of the same pitch, by definition, they don't even qualify as intervals. (The Harvard Dictionary Of Music defines the unison as a "pseudo-interval".)

So, if "perfect" intervals aren't perfect, one might ask: "Why do we continue to call them perfect?" I say it's because nobody has the guts to change their name. After all, who wants to set the whole music world on its ear by changing a term that's been around for over half of a millennium? Not me.

APPENDIX II
JAZZ/MODAL IMPROVISATION TRANSCRIPTIONS

EXAMPLE ONE

Goose Loose

EXAMPLE ONE

2 of 3

EXAMPLE ONE

3 of 3

APPENDIX II
JAZZ/MODAL IMPROVISATION TRANSCRIPTIONS

EXAMPLE TWO

EXAMPLE TWO

EXAMPLE TWO

EXAMPLE TWO

EXAMPLE TWO

D.S. al Coda

5 of 5

APPENDIX III
MUSIC STYLES/TYPES/PERIODS—CHECKLIST

Acid
Acid Rock
Advertisement
African
Aleatory
Allemande
Alternative
American
Anthem
Arcadian
Aria
Arioso
Art Rock
Atonal
Avant-Garde
_____

Ballad
Baroque
Beach
Bebop
Big Band
Birthday
Bitonal
Bluegrass
Blues
Bohemian
Boogie Woogie
Bop Jazz
Bossa Nova
Bourree
Brazilian
British
Broadway Show
_____

Cajun
Calypso
Canon
Cantata
Capriccio
Cha Cha
Chaconne
Chamber
Chance
Chanson

Chant
Chicago Blues
Choral
Chorale
Christmas
Classical
Classical/Popular
College
Commercial Jazz
Concerto
Contemporary
Contemp. Gospel
Contrapuntal
Cool Jazz
Country
Courante
Cowboy
Creole
_____

Dance
Dirge
Disco
Disney
Dixieland Jazz
Drinking
Duet
_____

Easy Listening
Eighty's
Electronic
Elevator
English
Ensemble
Ethnic
_____

Fanfare
Fantasia
Fantasy
Far Eastern
Festival
Fifty's
Finnish
Flamenco
Folk

Folk Rock
Forty's
Fox Trot
Free-Form Jazz
Free Jazz
French
Fugue
Funeral
Funk
Fusion
_____

Gavotte
German
Gigue
Gospel
Gregorian Chant
_____

Hard Bop
Hard Rock
Hawaiian
Heavy Metal
Hillbilly
Hip Hop
Homophonic
House
Hymn
_____

Impressionist
Impromptu
Improvisation
Indian
Industrial
Inspirational
Instrumental
Invention
Irish
Italian
_____

Jamaican
Jam Session
Jazz
Jazz Rock
Jewish
Jig

Lab Band
Latin
Latin Rhythm
Light Jazz
Liturgical
Local
_____

Madrigal
March
Mass
Mazurka
Medley
Metal
Military
Minuet
Modal
Modal Jazz
Mountain Music
Movie Theme
_____

Nationalist
Nature
Negro Spiritual
Neo-Classical
New Age
New Orleans Jazz
New Wave
New York Jazz
Ninety's
Northern
Norwegian
Novelty
Nursery
_____

Opera
Oratorio
Orchestral
Oriental
Original
Overture
_____

Parade
Passacaglia
Passion

Patriotic
Persian
Polka
Polonaise
Polyphonic
Pop Jazz
Popular
Prelude
Pre-Renaissance
Program
Progressive Jazz
Progressive Rock
Psychedelic Rock
Punk
_____

Quarter Tone
Quartet
Quintet
_____

Raga
Ragtime
Railroad
Rap
Recitative
Reggae
Regional
Religious
Renaissance
Requiem
Rhapsody
Rhumba
Rhythm & Blues
Rock
Rock 'n Roll
Rock-A-Billy
Romantic
Rondo
Russian
_____

Sacred
Samba
Saraband
Scherzo
Sea Shanty

Secular
Serenade
Serial
Seventy's
Sextet
Shag
Silence
Sing-A-Long
Sixty's
Ska
Skat
Slow Blues
Socca (Soka)
Solo
Sonata
Sonatina
Soul
Soundtrack
Southern
Southern Gospel
Spanish
Special Effect
Special Occasion
Spiritual
Stage Band
Standards
Stride
Suite
Surf
Swing
Symphonic
Symphonic Jazz
Symphonic Rock
_____

Techno
Tejano
Thanksgiving
Theme
Theme & Variations
Third Stream
Third World
Thirty's
Toccata
Tonal

Tone Poem
Traditional
Traditional Gospel
Trio
Tropical
TV Theme
Twelve-Bar Blues
Twelve Tone
Twentieth Century
Twenty's
_____

Viking
Vocal
_____

Waltz
Western
_____

Young Fogey
_____

Zydeco

INDEX

A

abstract reasoning, 2, 3
accelerando, 26, 30
accent mark, symbol defined, 30
accidentals, 10–11. *See also* flats; sharps
adagio, 30
adaptation, 178–80
ad lib, 30
Aebersold, Jamey, 211
Aeolian, 167, 168, 177
Alfred Publishing Company, 42
allegretto, 30
allegro, 30
altered tones, 139–41, 190
    pre-hearing, 188
    and scale degrees, 151
andante, 30
anticipation, 152, 162–63
appoggiatura, 152, 160–61, 166
arpeggiation method, 3, 60–62, 191
arpeggio, 60
"as written" approach, 1, 2, 5
    adaptation, 178–80
    advanced performance, 178
    instruction in, 213–15
    note reading methods, 7–10
    sight–reading, 2, 71–73
    transcription, 194–97
a tempo, 30
atonal music, 63
augmentation, 198, 205
augmented chords, 36, 38, 39
    figured bass, 96
    symbol, 47
    triads, 83
augmented intervals, 216
augmented mode, 168, 174, 177
aural ability
    aural memorization, 74
    in "chord symbol" approach, 3
    in "ear" approach, 4

aural training. *See* "ear" approach

B

bar lines, 11, 19
    bass in playing by ear, 123, 124, 125
    in three hand method, 48, 58–59
bass clef
    counting, 21
    figured bass, 96
    slogans for, 8
    staff, 6
    in two hand method, 46
beats
    counting, 20–24
    strong and weak beats, 152, 153
Belwin Mills, 15, 42
Belwin Piano Method, 15
bird's eye, 31
black notes, 6
blues music, 173–74, 227
bridge, 120

C

canon, 207
cantabile, 30
chords, 35–39, 82–89. *See also* seventh
    chords; triads
    altered scale degree chords, 104–5
    altered tones, 139–41
    augmented, 36, 38, 39, 47, 83, 96
    aural training, 40–41
    chord members, 36–39, 86, 208
    damper pedals used in playing, 28
    defined, 35–36
    diatonic seventh chord exercise, 178–79
    diminished. *See* diminished chords
    false root, 88, 101
    figured bass, 96–97, 99–100
    implying harmony, 130
    major, 36–37, 38, 47, 83
    minor, 36, 38, 47, 83
    mutations, 101–7
    pivot chords, 108

chords, *(continued)*
   principal, 97, 99
   replacement, 99
   and scales, 128–30
   special instruction chords, 86–88,
      131–38
   suspended chord, 87
   types, 36–39, 85
   voicing, 128, 208
chord scales, 89
   chord voicing, 128
   improvisation, 181–85, 192
"chord symbol" approach 1, 3, 180–85
   adaptation, 178–80
   arpeggiation method, 3, 60–62, 191
   chord scale improvisation, 181–85, 192
   combining with other approaches, 5,
      213–15
   finger exercise, 54–60
   harmonization, 118–19
   in inversion form, 49–54
   non–harmonic tone improvisation,
      186–93
   three hand method, 3, 48–60
   transcription, 194–97
   two hand method, 3, 45–48
chord symbols
   abbreviations of chords, 85
   numbers in, 87–88
   root position, 49–50, 52, 53, 60
chromatic line, 110
circle of fifths, 89–92
   in analyzing harmony, 100
   application of, 95
classical music, 227
   in "as written" approach, 2
   development in, 120
   dotted eighth sixteenth notes in, 43–44
   independence between hands in, 77
   intermediate level, 42

use of thematic development devices, 198
coda, 30, 120
common tones, 98
composite melody, 198, 208
composition, 111–21
   "as written" harmonization, 114–18
   chord symbol harmonization, 118–19
   development, 120
   harmony, 114–20
   maintaining balance in, 209–11
   melody, 111–14
   songform, 119–20
con brio, 30
consonance, in intervals, 217. *See also*
      dissonance
contemporary gospel music
   special instruction chords, 131–38
counter melody, 198, 206
crescendo, 26, 30
Cristofori, Bartolommeo, 212
cross rhythm, 198, 203. *See also* hemiola
cut, symbol defined, 30
cut time, symbol defined, 30
D
da capo, 30
dal segno, 30
damper pedal, 28–29
   in three hand method, 56, 58
D.C. al fine, 30
D.C. (da capo), 30, 72
decrescendo, 26, 30
descant, 198, 207
descant line, 123
development, 120. *See also* thematic
      development
diatonic seventh chord exercise, 178–79
diminished chords, 36, 38, 39
   figured bass symbols, 96
   modulation, use in, 111
   symbol, 47
   tonic triad, 171

diminished chords *(continued)*
    triads, 83
diminished intervals, 82, 88, 216
diminished mode, 168, 175, 177
diminuendo, 30
diminution, 198, 204
dissonance, 208. *See also* consonance
    Gb pentatonic and lack of, 172–73
    in intervals, 217
    in non-harmonic tones, 152–67, 187–88
divided line, 42–43, 206
Dobbins, Bill, 211
Dorian, 167, 168, 169–70, 177, 194
dotted notes
    dotted eighth sixteenths, 43–44
    in rhythm level charts, 20, 21, 22, 23
double bar, 31
double mordent, 80
A Dozen A Day, 15, 42
D.S. al coda, 30
D.S. (dal segno), 30, 72
duple time, 195
duration, 63

E
"ear" approach, 1, 4, 122–27
    advanced, 194–211
    ear training, 40–41, 194
    instruction in, 213–15
    lowered intervals, 122
    pre-hearing, 185–86, 188
    transcription, 194–97
Edna Mae Burnam's Piano Course, 15
eighth notes, 21, 22, 23
embellishments, 78–81
escape tones, 152, 158–59, 167
exercises. *See also* practice
    analyzing harmony, 99–101
    "as written" harmonization, 114–18
    balance exercise, 76–77
    basic techniques, 15–28
    chord position finger exercise, 54–60

circle of fifths, 95
    diatonic seventh chord exercise, 178–79
    ear training, 123–27
    figured bass, 101
    marathon scale, 71
    non–harmonic tone improvisation, 188–91
    rhythmic transcription, 195–96
extension, 198, 200, 209

F
fake sheets, 46
false roots, 88, 101
fermata, 31
figured bass, 89, 96–97
    application of, 99–101
    in determining harmony, 124
    in harmonization, 115–18
    mutations, 101–7
    for transposition, 107
fine, 31
fingering
    basic practice techniques, 18
    chord position exercises, 54–60
    chords, 36
    embellishments, 78
    major scales, 14
    minor seventh chord, 84
    muscle memory, 74
    practice, 17–18, 25
    seventh chords, 83–84
    in a theme, 113–14
    three hand method, 52–54
    two hand method, 47
finger numbers, 14, 64–70
first ending, symbol defined, 31.
flash cards, note reading aid, 10
flats
    in circle of fifths, 89, 90–92
    in determining key signature, 95
    learning to read, 10–11
forte, symbol defined, 31
fortissimo, symbol defined, 31

G

glide, 78

glissando, 78

grace note, 78

grand staff, 7. *See also* staff

grave, 31

grazioso, 31

Gregorian chant, 194, 227

H

half notes, 20, 21, 22, 23

hand positions. *See also* left hand; right hand

    basic practice techniques, 16–20

    chord position finger exercise, 54–59

    playing scales, 14, 64–70

    technical exercises, 76–77

    three hand method, 48–49, 56, 57

    two hand method, 48

harmonic minor, 177

harmonization

    "as written" harmonization, 114–18

    "chord symbol" harmonization, 118–19

    figured bass in, 115–18

harmony, 35. *See also* chords

    adding to theme, 113

    analyzing, 99–101

    "chord symbol" playing, 3

    composing, 114–20

    implied by chords, 130

    and melody, 137–38

    non-harmonic tones, 152–67

    playing by ear, 123, 124–25, 126

    playing over chords, 54–57

    quartal, 128

    and right hand, 17

    secundal, 128

    tertian, 128–29

    in three hand method, 48–60

    in two hand method, 45, 47

hemiola, 198, 203. *See also* cross rhythm

hold symbol, 31

hymn music, 72, 227

I

improvisation, 227

    chord scale, 181–85

    "chord symbol" approach, 3

    development in, 120

    "ear" approach, 4

    jazz/modal improvisation, 128, 194–208, 219–26

    modes and, 167–68

    non-harmonic tone improvisation, 186–93

    use of thematic development devices, 198

instruction

    approaches to, 213–15

    jazz study, 211

    piano lessons, 33–34

interlude, 120

intervals

    augmentation, 205

    augmented, 216

    classification, 216–18

    defined, 35

    diminished, 82, 216

    diminution, 204

    lowered, 82, 122

    major, 216

    minor, 82, 216

    octaves, 35, 58, 70

    perfect, 35, 82, 216, 217–18

    sound qualities of, 40, 122

introduction, 120

inversions, 49–54, 101, 197, 198–99

inverted diminished mode, 168, 175–76, 177

inverted mordent, 80

Ionian (major mode), 167, 168, 177

J

jazz/modal improvisation

    advanced ear training, 194–208

    chord voicing, 128

    transcription examples, 219–26

jazz music
    altered minor mode in, 176, 177
    eleventh scale degree in, 146
    further study of, 211
    jazz/modal improvisation in, 128,
        194–208, 219–26
    Locrian mode in, 171, 177
    Lydian mode in, 170, 177
    modes used in, 177
    Phrygian mode in, 170–71, 177
    special instruction chords, 131–38
jump-cut, 108–11

K
key
    determining, 94–95, 124
    minor key, 102–4
    modulation, 107–11
    mutations, 101–7
    keyboard chart, note reading method, 7
key signatures, 14, 19, 48
    circle of fifths, 89–92, 95
    and Dorian mode, 170
    relative minor/relative major, 92–94

L
Lanning, Russell E., 42
largo, 31
lead sheets, 46, 107
leap progression, 153, 158–59
ledger line, 6
left hand
    abbreviation defined, 31
    ability of, 17
    in arpeggiation, 62
    chord voicing, 208
    in major scales, 14
    in two hand method, 45, 47
legato, 31
lento, 31
lessons. *See* instruction
Levine, Mark, 211
L.H. (left hand), 31. *See also* left hand

line notes, 1
    middle C, 6
    in note relationships, 8–9
    numbering, 7
Locrian, 168, 171–72, 177
lowered intervals, 82, 122
Lydian, 167, 168, 177

M
major
    chords, 36–37, 38, 47
    intervals, 216
    mode (Ionian), 167, 168, 177
    relative minor/relative major, 92–94
    scales, 96
    seventh chords, 83, 84, 85, 122
marcato, 31
measure, 19, 20
Mehegan, John, 211
melodic minor, 177
melody. *See also* intervals
    augmentation, 205
    "chord symbol" playing, 3
    composing, 111–14
    damper pedals used in, 28
    defined, 35
    diminution, 204
    and harmony, 137–38
    implied by scales, 130
    playing by ear, 123–25
    playing over chords, 54–57
    repetition, 201
    and right hand, 16–17
    thematic development devices, 197–208
    three hand method, 48
    two hand method, 45–46, 48
memorization, 73–75
meno, 31
metronomes
    basic practice techniques, 24
    intermediate practice, 47
    practice strategies, 32

metronomes *(continued)*
    scales practice, 71
mezzo-forte, symbol defined, 31
mezzo-piano, symbol defined, 31
Michael Aaron Piano Course, 15, 42
middle C, 6
minor
    chords, 36, 38, 47, 83, 96–97
    forms of, 102–4
    intervals, 82, 216
    relative minor/relative major, 92–94
    scales, 67–70
    seventh chords, 83, 84, 85, 122
mixolydian, 167, 168–69, 177, 194
mnemonic devices
    slogans and note reading method, 8
modes, 89, 167–76, 194. *See also* major;
    minor
    altered blues, 168, 177
    altered minor, 168, 176, 177
    altered pentatonic, 168, 177
    blues, 168, 173–74, 177
    diminished, 168, 175, 177
    inverted diminished mode, 168, 175–76,
177
    mutations, 101–7
    whole tone, 168, 174, 177
modulation, 107–11
mordent, 80
motive, 112. *See also* theme
Music by the Masters, 42
music composition. *See* composition
Musicord Publications, 42
mutations, 101–7, 109, 125
    altered scale degrees, 104–5
    examples, 102
    minor forms, 102–4
    secondary dominant, 105–7

N

natural minor mode (Aeolian), 167, 168,
    177

naturals, 10–11
N.C. (no chord), 86, 88
Neapolitan chord, 105
neighbor tones, 152, 156–57, 166
no chord. *See* N. C. (no chord)
non-harmonic tone improvisation, 128, 186–93
non-harmonic tones, 89, 152–67
    anticipation, 152, 162–63
    appoggiatura, 152, 160–61, 166
    escape tones, 152, 158–59, 167
    neighbor tones, 152, 156–57, 166
    passing tones, 152, 154–55, 166
    suspension, 152, 164–65
note reading, 1, 7–10. *See also* "as written"
    approach; sight-reading
    keyboard chart, 7
    note relationships, 8–9
    slogans, 8
notes. *See also* note values
    basic practice techniques, 16–17
    embellishments, 78–81
    fill notes, 59
    line note, 1
    mistakes in playing, 25–26
    note patterns, 16, 25
    reading notes. *See* note reading
    relationship between notes, 8–9
    in rhythm charts, 19–23
    space note, 1, 7, 8–9
    in time signatures, 20
note values
    defined, 20
    dotted eighth sixteenth notes, 43–44
    dotted notes, 20, 21, 22, 23
    eighth notes, 21, 22, 23
    half notes, 20, 21, 22, 23
    quarter notes, 20, 21, 22, 23
    triplets, 44–45
    whole notes, 20, 21, 22, 23

O

octave and fifth, 62
octaves, 35
    scales, 70
    three hand method, 58
oriental music, 227
oriental sound
    and pentatonic mode, 173
ornaments, 78–81
outer voices, 123

P

pantonal music, 63
partridges, in pear trees, 90
passing tone, 152, 154–55, 166
patterns, 73, 74–75
pedals, 28–29
pentatonic, 168, 172–73, 177
perfect intervals, 35, 82, 216, 217–18
performance, 2, 215
Persian music, 228
    diminished mode in, 175
    inverted diminished mode in, 176
phrasing, 26, 27
Phrygian, 167, 168, 170–71, 177
piano, history of, 212
piano students. *See* students
piano teachers. *See* teachers
Picardy third, 93, 100
pitch, 63
pivot chords, 108–11
poco a poco, 31
polka, 152, 228
polyphonic thematic development devices,
    206–8
popular music, 228
    "chord symbol" approach, 3
    development in, 120
    dotted eighth sixteenth notes in, 43–44
    and mixolydian mode, 168
practice. *See also* exercises
    basic techniques, 15–28

beginning level music, 15
    defined, 15–16
    four octave scales, 71
    intermediate performance, 42
    memorization, 73–75
    sight-reading, 71–73
    strategies, 32
    tips for parents, 33–34
presto, 31
primary dominants, 105
principal chords, 97, 99

Q

quartal harmony, 128
quarter notes, 20, 21, 22, 23

R

ragtime music, 2, 228
relative minor/relative major, 92–94
repeat sign, 31, 72
repetition, 198, 201, 209
resolution, 186–88, 192
rests, 19–23
retrograde, 197, 199
retrograde inversion, 197, 199
R.H. (right hand), 31. *See also* right hand
rhythm, 35
    augmentation, 205
    basic practice techniques, 19–24, 25–26
    "chord symbol" playing, 3
    defined, 39
    diminution, 204
    repetition, 201
    transcription of, 194–96
rhythm level charts, 19–23
right hand
    abbreviation defined, 31
    in major scales, 14
    and melody, 16–17
    in two hand method, 45–46
ritard, 26, 31
rock music, 152, 194, 228
roll, 79

root positions
    in chord position finger exercise, 54
    in three hand approach, 49–53, 60
round, 207
S
scale degrees, 97–99
    altered scale degree chords, 104–5
    altered tones, 151
    pentatonic mode, 172–73
    primary dominant, 98, 105
    secondary dominant, 105–7
    tendencies and qualities of, 141–51
scales, 63–71, 167
    and chords, 128–30
    described, 12
    finger numbers, 14
    implying melody, 130
    major scales, 12–13, 64–67
    minor scales, 67–70
    scale degrees. *See* scale degrees
scherzando, 31
secondary dominants, 105–7
second ending, symbol defined, 31
secundal harmony, 128
segno, symbol defined, 31
self-discipline, 3
sempre, 31
sequencing, 198, 202
seventh chords, 83–84, 85
    aural distinction of, 122
    diatonic seventh chords exercise, 178–79
    dominant seventh chords, 83–84, 85,
        106, 122
    major seventh, 83, 84, 85
    minor seventh, 83, 84, 85
    tendencies of, 85
    in three hand method, 53
sforzando, symbol defined, 31
shading, 26–28
sharps
    in circle of fifths, 89, 90–92

    in determining key signature, 94
    learning to read, 10–11
sight-reading, 2, 71–73. *See also* "as
        written" approach; note reading
simile, 31
slight accent, symbol defined, 31
slogans, note reading method, 8
slurs, 27
Small, Allan, 42
songform, 119–20
space notes, 1
    in note relationships, 8–9
    numbering, 7
special instruction chords, 86–88, 131–38
staccato, 31
staff
    bass clef staff, 6
    divided line, 42
    grand staff, 7
    treble clef staff, 6
step progression, 153
    and appoggiatura, 160–61
    and neighbor tones, 156–57
    and passing tones, 154–55
stretto, 198, 207
strong accent, symbol defined, 30
students
    author's letter to, 213–15
    note to parents of, 33–34
style (mode of expression), 26
styles of music, 227–28
suspended chord, 87
suspension, 152, 164–65
symbols
    defined, 30–31
    for embellishments, 78–81
    in figured bass, 96–97, 115–18
    number of, written in rhythm charts, 20, 22,
        23
    special instruction chord symbols, 86
syncopation, 152–53

T
teachers, 2
    author's letter to, 213–15
    limitations of, 5, 213
    and practice, 15, 213
Teacher's Choice for the Young Pianist,
    42
teaching. *See* instruction
technique, 75–76
tempo, 31
terminology, 30–31
tertian harmony, 128–29
thematic development devices, 197–208
themes, 113. *See also* motive
    songform, 119–20
    thematic development devices, 197–208
three hand method, 3, 48–60, 191
    bass line, 48, 58–59
    in chord scale improvisation, 181–85
    inversion, 49–54
    melody over chord, 54–57
    root position, 49, 60
ties, 27, 164
time signatures, 19–20, 23, 195
tonal music, 63, 228
to next strain, 31
tonic chords, 100
transcription, 194–97, 208
    jazz/modal improvisation, 197, 219–26
    of rhythm, 194–96
transposition
    figured bass for, 107
treble clef
    counting, 21
    slogans for, 8
    staff, 6
    in two hand method, 46
tremolo, 79
triads, 38, 83, 97–98. *See also* chords
    aural distinction of, 40–41
    diminished, 88

dominant, 98, 106
subdominant, 98
in three hand method, 52
tonic, 97–98, 100, 171
trill, 79
triple time, 195
triplets, 44–45
truncation, 198, 200
turn, 80
two hand method, 3, 45–48, 191
V
vivace, 31
voices
    outer and inner, 123
voicing, 128, 208
W
white notes, 6
whole notes, 20, 21, 22, 23
Willis Music Company, 15, 42